A GRUMPY MAN'S GUIDE TO SUBURBIA

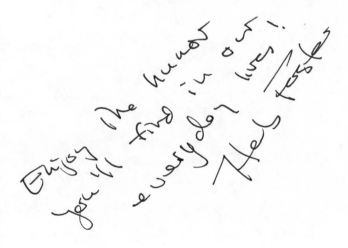

Enjoy the humor
you'll find in our
everyday lives!

Herb Fosler

A GRUMPY MAN'S GUIDE TO SUBURBIA

ON MARRIAGE, KIDS, CHORES, AND MORE

BY HERB FOSTER

COSIMO-ON-DEMAND

NEW YORK

A Grumpy Man's Guide to Suburbia

© 2005 by Herb Foster

ISBN: 1-59605-774-2

These columns originally appeared in *The Record-Review* or the *Patent Trader* newspapers.

Cosimo
P.O. Box 416
Old Chelsea Station
New York, NY 10113-0416

or visit our Web site at:
www.cosimobooks.com

Library of Congress Cataloging-in-Publication Data
A catalog record for this book is available from the Library of Congress

Cover illustration by Roger Raymond
Cover design by www.wiselephant.com

With deep appreciation and love,

To Tina, who not only has put up with me for all these years but also has been the subject of more columns than she wanted,

To the boys (see above),

To Murphy and Maddy and all the dogs over the years,

To Jane, Liz, RJ, and all the other editors who corrected my bad grammar and spelling,

And anyone else I missed, and with my memory, I am sure there are plenty.

CONTENTS

Like Most Men

All Tie'd Up

Like most men, I have 247 ties. I wear eight on a regular basis.

These facts by themselves are not a problem to me. What makes them a problem is my wife. About two or three times a year, she goes on a tirade that sounds something like this: "You have 8,000 ties. Your closet is a mess. You have ties dating back to your fifth-grade choir recital! Some of your ties have collected more food than our refrigerator. Go through your ties and throw away a few. Or better yet, give them to the Salvation Army—if they'll take them!"

What she doesn't understand is that I have valid reasons for keeping my ties. To demonstrate this to my wife, and to keep the peace, I recently took all my ties out of the closet and laid them out on the bed. Here's what I found:

1. The Eight Current Favorites. This is the Varsity. These I wear all the time. Actually, this is not a static group. If I get bored with a favorite, or it gets hurt in battle (stained), it gets benched.

2. Thirty-five ties that are strong contenders for the "favorites" group. These are frequently taken out of the closet, held up next to a suit, and then put back. I think of these as Junior Varsity ties, eager to jump into the starting lineup if chili or vegetable soup attacks a member of the Varsity.

3. Thirty-eight that were former Varsity All-Stars but now are past their prime and haven't gotten much action over the past few years. I still have great fondness for them and can't throw them away. They have served me well, and I might wear them again. I really might.

4. Sixteen ties that I didn't even know I had, and now that I've found them, I'm going to strongly consider them for the starting squad.

5. Twelve very wide ties that look like lobster bibs. These have gone out of fashion, but the style might come back. My wife can't tell me

to discard these ties. She herself uses this rationale to explain why she has 10,000 pairs of shoes.

6. Fourteen very narrow ties (see above).

7. Twenty-six bow ties. I have stopped wearing bow ties in general (they make me look like Orville Redenbacher), but I still like them, and they don't take up much space in the closet.

8. Sixteen gift ties. Most of these are purple and orange paisley patterns. I wouldn't wear them to shovel manure in the garden. However, they were gifts from important people in my life (my wife, my mother, my sister, my wife), so I'd better not throw them away.

9. Eight dirty ties. These were once current favorites that became spotted or frayed. I keep them because I once loved them, and I can always wear them to a cocktail party with a sweater or vest.

10. Nine summer ties. These are light pink or yellow and can be worn only in the warmer months. Of course, when summer comes, they are buried so deep under the winter ties that I can't find them.

11. Six school ties. Two from my school, and one each from my father's college, my father-in-law's college, my son's college, and of course, my Viking Victory tie from Camp KatchaWooket. How could I throw that away?

12. Ten "special occasion" ties. One has dirty words in small type. One is pink, with a sexy lady in a palm tree. These are great for costume parties or when I feel a bit frisky. Actually, what usually happens is I try them on, decide they are too frisky, and go back to the Varsity.

13. One string tie. This came from our family trip out West. It carries fond memories, and I save it in case I get invited to a Western dress-up party.

14. Four holiday ties. One has Santa on skis. One has turkeys. They get one wearing a year then go back on the rack.

15. Twenty-seven miscellaneous. These are ties that I couldn't put in any category but couldn't bear to throw away.

For those of you counting, note that I've reached a total of 242 and, indeed, have discovered my wife was right. I have five ties that I don't need. Two were ironed by the dry cleaners and have shiny ridges running down the front. Two are badly frayed and faded, and the last one is a narrow knit tie, bright red.

With great pride, I marched these into my wife. "See, I am throwing away five ties," I said, expecting great praise. Instead, I got the opposite: "You have 5,000 ties. You spend three hours going through them, and only throw away five! *Men!*" She threw the ties in the air and stomped from the room.

I was going to chase her and explain why I was keeping the other 242, but I didn't. For one thing, I was a little tired after sorting all my ties; also, I was looking at the red tie on the floor. Maybe I should keep it.

Shopping for Your Wife Made Easy!

The holidays are a very stressful time for men. Although they usually only need to shop for one person, it is very difficult to find an appropriate gift for that one person.

Many a man has endured extreme frigid temperatures for prolonged periods based on a poor gift-buying decision at this time of year. Many men cook Sunday-night dinners for months because of their failure to come up with a meaningful token of their appreciation.

Being a veteran of these wars over the years and having made a few mistakes myself, I am happy to pass on advice to my brothers in arms.

PRESENTS NOT TO BUY YOUR WIFE

Don't buy anything that plugs in. As a general rule, anything that requires electricity is seen as utilitarian and therefore is not perceived as a "gift." This especially applies to items such as washing machines, dishwashers, irons, etc. For some reason, wives tend to think of these as not very romantic.

Don't buy anything that involves weight loss or self-improvement. For example, a six-month membership in the Diet Center or Weight Watchers could be perceived by your spouse as a criticism or suggestion that she might be overweight. Your intentions might be good, and your wife might be saying, "I need to go to the Diet Center," but I would definitely avoid this gift.

Don't buy clothes that involve sizes. The chances are one in seven million that you will get the size right, and your wife will be offended the other 6,999,999 times. "Do I look like a size 16?" is what she'll say. Too small a size doesn't cut it either: "I haven't worn a size 8 in 20 years. Did you have to remind me?"

Avoid all things that are useful. I realize you need a new mirror in the bathroom, but it is probably not a good idea to wrap this up and put it under the tree. The new silver polish you saw advertised might, indeed, save hundreds of hours of scrubbing, but it's not going to win you any brownie points when presented with gift wrapping and a bow.

The same is true of gadgets, tools, and car accessories. For some strange reason that men cannot comprehend, women don't seem to have the same appreciation for motors and TV accessories that we do. Definitely avoid buying that new TV universal remote that makes it easier to watch multiple sports events at the same time.

Don't buy jewelry. Let me tell you from experience: the jewelry your wife wants, you can't afford. The jewelry you can afford, your wife doesn't want. Don't go there!

Do not buy something that involves your hobby. If you are a fly-fisherman, don't present a collection of new flies from Harry's Bait and Tackle. If you are a golfer, I'd skip the new video on *How to Improve Your Swing*. If she hasn't picked up your hobby, she won't appreciate your thoughtfulness.

And guys, do not, I repeat, DO NOT, fall into the traditional trap of buying your wife frilly underwear. Your idea of the kind of underwear your wife should wear and what she actually wears are light-years apart. (Most of these things are sexy but very uncomfortable. Well, that's what I've been told, anyway.) Almost every woman has a drawer full of unworn undergarments purchased by their husbands, and these things aren't returnable, fellas.

Don't spend too much, whatever you do. You will get yelled at. "How do you think we're going to pay for that?" On the other hand, don't spend too little. She won't say anything, but she'll think: "Is that all I'm worth?"

I realize I have offered a lot of advice on what *not* to buy for your wife but nothing on what *to buy*. As I said, the holidays are a very stressful time of year.

Where There's Smoke

The last true bastion of male chauvinism is not the golf course or the poker table but the barbecue. I've seen women beat men at golf, and I have seen a man cook dinner, but I have never attended a dinner party where a woman cooked out on the grill.

During the summer, we frequently witness a traditional ritual at cookouts. People arrive, have cocktails, eat hors d'oeuvres, and mingle until the grill is started. Then the men begin to act differently. Slowly, they begin to gather around the fire, drinks in hand, leaning slightly backward, watching their host closely.

They are not drawn to the fire by primitive instincts. They are drawn by the challenge. Here is another guy about to show his stuff, and they want to see competitive technique. By custom, it's considered bad form to offer an opinion or criticize, unless, of course, the griller pokes the meat with a fork and says something like: "What do you think?" Then it's open season for all observers.

One person will immediately ask, "How long has it been on?" Another will take the fork and press down on the meat. A third will say, "The flames aren't high enough." They are representatives of distinct styles of barbecuing, and believe me, there are several marked schools of thought on the subject.

TIMERS: These people put the meat on and leave it for a specified period of time without touching it. "Eight minutes each side," they say, and check their watch frequently to make sure they are on schedule. They are so confident of their technique that they never check the meat until their clock says it is done.

POKERS: This group can tell how well meat or chicken is done "by feel." They take a large fork—or worse, their fingers!—and frequently push down in the center of the meat to check for firmness.

SPLASHERS: Armed with a paintbrush or baster, Splashers cover anything that gets near the grill with some kind of sauce. They put teriyaki on steak, mustard on chops, and barbecue mix on ribs. They are like artists, painting constantly throughout the cooking process.

CUTTERS: At regular intervals during the cooking process, these people cut the meat to see how it is doing. By the time the meat is served, it looks as if it was attacked by Edward Scissorhands.

SEARERS: This sect believes that high heat seals in the flavor. High heat translates to high flames, so this cook is frequently seen working in front of a major bonfire. Some people call this group "Burners" rather than Searers, and you can usually pick this type out of a crowd by their thin eyebrow hair.

CONSTANT MOVERS: This group cannot leave anything on the grill alone. They are constantly moving, turning, poking, lifting, etc. They adjust the flame at least ten times while cooking one hamburger. This group I classify as the A.D.D. Chef clan.

And there are Hybrid Grillers. Say, a Splasher/Cutter. This person will put sauce all over the meat for most of the cooking process and then turn into a cutter near the end, slashing away at the meat. When the final product is served, it is truly unrecognizable—covered with a thick sauce and ribbed with deep gashes. Or the Searer/Splasher. This person turns the meat into a dark black chunk of charcoal and then hides it under a thick coating of sauce.

Recently, when I had friends over, I made the mistake of asking the gathered experts for advice. Almost immediately, a debate broke out between two of the men who have opposing styles—a Timer and a Constant Mover. They practically dueled it out with a fork and a spatula.

I went to get salt and pepper, and when I returned, I couldn't get near my own grill. Since I had trouble seeing over the group gathered around, offering advice, I retreated to the porch. There I found all the wives, having a lovely time, waiting for the outcome of the grill battle. It was a quiet, peaceful scene, overlooking the ruckus out on the lawn.

You don't suppose women have been encouraging men to cook out all these years for an ulterior motive? You don't suppose they could actually cook on the grill as well as men do? No, I must be dreaming. Men must really be superior at cooking on the barbecue.

Tina's on Tuesday

Now that I'm writing for a newspaper on a regular basis, I have a new career goal. I want to secure one of the great jobs of all time: restaurant critic. Imagine—dining in a fancy eatery and not having to pay for it, stuffing yourself with big steaks and rich desserts, putting the cost on your expense report, and getting to say that you were only doing your job!

As a restaurant critic, you also have the last say. If the waiter ignores you for hours, or the bartender is rude, then you can zap them in your review with a reference to the questionable service or staff attitude. If the steak sauce is too spicy, you don't need to send it back, just give it no stars. What a wonderful job!

However, I realize I have no track record in this field, so to achieve my goal, I've decided to sharpen my skills by reviewing a meal served at home by my wife.

Rating: ★★

The restaurant is set in a lovely old colonial-style house, slightly tattered around the edges, but clean and charming in its own way. We were greeted at the door by a large tail-wagging Labrador retriever, making us feel warm and welcome.

The simplistic "California" influence of this establishment can be seen immediately, as very little effort was made on presentation. The plain kitchen table, the silverware piled in the middle, and the folded paper towel for napkins were startling at first but communicated clearly that this was a straightforward, no-nonsense eatery.

Appetizers consisted of raw vegetables on a paper plate, lacking in presentation but fresh and tasty. The stark contrast of white cardboard with the colorful vegetables clearly marked this eatery with the minimalist approach of Nouvelle Cuisine.

The main course, the meat, was prepared in cylindrical fashion, about four inches long and served nicely browned with a moist tender center. It was topped by a lightly textured brown sauce, with a spicy aftertaste, and placed in a pastry-type shell. I found the shell disappointing, flaky on the outside but doughy inside, and recommend that the pastry chef strive for greater consistency.

A highlight of the meal was the crispy *pommes de terre*, cut into thin strips, and prepared with a tangy, red, tomato-based dressing. While a touch greasy, they were flavorful and succulent.

Tina's has a unique way of serving dessert, which was ice cream in a cookie-like shell. The owner/manager stands in the kitchen and yells "Catch!" then tosses the dessert to each diner. Startling but innovative, this twist was in keeping with Tina's overall laid-back style.

The atmosphere of the establishment left something to be desired. Watching two boys, ten and six, stick their tongues out at each other was not suitable entertainment to accompany fine dining, but the hostess/manager was able to solve this problem with a flick of her hand.

This restaurant would be worth four stars if it weren't for the service. The waitress constantly ignored my wineglass, forcing me to refill it myself from the bottle, and only by raising my voice at the six-year-old was I able to get my place setting cleared.

Overall, I'd recommend Tina's on Tuesday, but reservations are an absolute must. The management has been known to get upset when unannounced diners arrive, or when someone with a reservation fails to show up, as has happened to this reviewer on several occasions.

★★

Now that I have written my first review, I'm hoping the editor will offer me an immediate position. In the meantime, I will keep practicing. Perhaps I'll try Wendy's on Wednesday or Sarah's on Saturday. I think I'll start calling my friends to see if they would welcome my services as a food critic.

A Husband's Prerogative

Here is my question for the day: Is it ever acceptable to lie to your wife? No, of course not, you say. A marriage is based on truth, on trust, on a foundation of 100 percent honesty. It is never acceptable to lie to your wife.

Does this apply to white lies? Or answers that are incomplete or don't exactly tell the entire story? No, again, you tell me, this is not permissible. You must be fully forthright at all times.

Now, I understand all of this, but let me give you some situations that put this belief in question:

- Your wife goes away for the weekend to visit her mother. Friday night, you have the boys over to play poker, and you eat hot chicken wings, drink beer, and make rude remarks all night. Saturday, you watch sports with your feet on the couch and eat all the fattening food she won't allow in the house. On Sunday when she returns, she says: "Did you miss me?"

- You're getting dressed to go out, and your wife is looking in the mirror. She turns to you and bluntly asks, "Am I getting heavy?"

- You're sitting on the beach, and a beautiful woman in a string bikini walks by. You watch intently, a number of thoughts running through your head. Your spouse turns to you and says, "Were you looking at her?"

- You're forty-five minutes late for a social event, and your bride is trying on the seventy-eighth outfit, which looks to you pretty much the same as the previous seventy-seven. She finally comes out, does a little spin, and asks, "Do you like this better?"

- It's a Saturday afternoon, and you are stretched out on the couch, thinking about a little nap, when your wife comes in an says, "I just invited Julie and Tom and their four kids over. Is that OK?"

You know what I am talking about? When a woman asks these questions, the time is not right for a man to do his George Washington "I'll never tell a lie" routine and speak the truth. If you do, the woman will just break out in tears and say, "You don't love me!"

Now I don't want to be perceived as advocating lying, but I think men should get a little leeway—call it a Husband's Prerogative. This wouldn't cover serious things like having an affair or stealing money out of her pocketbook, but it would cover harmless situations where the truth might not be the best course of action.

The primary criteria for exercising a Husband's Prerogative would be: Will your marriage be better off if you tell the truth? For example, you're outside working in the garden with your wife when your neighbor calls to ask if you can come over and help him with a project. You go over, the project takes five minutes, and then the two of you have a beer and watch the ball game for an hour or so. When you come back, your wife says, "That must have been some project!" You have two possible answers: 1) "Yes, dear, it was," or 2) "Actually, I've been drinking beer and watching the ball game with Sam." Now, which do you think is the best answer?

Here's another example: Your wife goes antiquing and comes home with some blue china bowls, which she thinks are "adorable." She asks if you like them. Truthfully, you don't give one hoot about china, especially an old, not-useful bowl with unknown heritage. But do you tell her that? Of course not! You say you "love them."

If your wife spends hours cooking a meal, it doesn't matter if it tastes like old sneakers with saddle-soap sauce; the Husband's Prerogative ensures that the words that come out of your mouth are things like "spectacular" and "a gourmet's delight."

How about this one? Her mother calls and asks if "that strong husband of yours" will help move a solid-oak dresser and "a few other little things." Your wife asks, "You don't mind, do you?" You think about your aching back, but your Husband's Prerogative allows you to say "I'd love to!"

Or she comes home with new shoes. They are blue with straps

and look identical to several hundred other pairs already residing in her closet. When she asks, "Aren't these a great buy?" the Husband's Prerogative forces words out of your mouth like: "I don't know how you do it. What a great shopper you are!"

Of course, some people may wonder if it is always appropriate to utilize the Husband's Prerogative in these kinds of situations. I suggest that the best way to determine this is to ask yourself: "Does she really want to hear the truth?" "Does she really want to hear that she is getting heavy?" "Does she care what you think of her china or her shoes?" Of course not! She expects her husband to exercise his Husband's Prerogative, and you shouldn't disappoint her.

Food for Thought

One of the frictions in a marriage is a man's performance of domestic duties. Women frequently complain that their husbands can't even do a simple job like the grocery shopping. But I maintain that it is the woman's fault. She sends the male into that supermarket maze without proper instructions, and she has unrealistic expectations concerning his performance.

So, to ease this friction, and as a public service to women everywhere, I have decided to publish:

THE DO'S AND DON'TS OF SENDING YOUR HUSBAND TO THE SUPERMARKET

1. Always send him with a written list. If you give him vague instructions like, "Run down and pick up something for dinner," he will return with eight bags of groceries full of things like chips, dips, snack food, beer, ice cream, and the like, but NO DINNER.

2. Be very specific with your list. Do not write down a vague word like "vegetables" because a man thinks that pickles and olives are vegetables. (They *are* green.)

3. Be clear about the size and amount of whatever it is you need, and include what degree of variance you will accept. If your list does not say "tomato sauce—8 oz—no bigger than 16 oz," then your husband will bring home the two-gallon size of tomato sauce because it was on sale, and he saved eight cents. (He'll be proud of himself, too!)

4. Include a list of things he CANNOT buy. Your list should say "NO summer sausage!" "NO hot dogs in blankets." "NO frozen jalapeño poppers." Of course, the man will not be able to resist a few of these items, but this tactic usually limits the damage.

5. Don't assume he knows anything. If you write down "soap"

thinking he will know what kind of soap he has been washing with for several years, you have made a mistake. He has no idea. He might know it is green or white, but even that is questionable.

6. Give the man visual hints if possible. Write: "Tide = big red bottle with white top (don't buy blue top). Should be on bottom shelf." Of course, there is the chance that he will buy the white bottle with the red top, but you've done your best.

7. Realize that a man has limitations and don't ask him to buy something complicated. For example, don't put "Arid Extra Dry" on the list. The man will get to the supermarket and discover that there are twenty-eight varieties of Arrid Extra Dry, all in containers that look similar. He will find that all the sizes look alike and the names—Fresh, Outdoor Fresh, and Fresh Unscented—are very close. He'll just grab whatever is closest to his hand, and you will be disappointed.

8. Never ask a man to buy fruit. What he brings home will be either rock hard or near rotten. Determining if a cantaloupe is ready for consumption is way beyond a man's capabilities.

9. Do not ask him to pick up any kind of feminine product. The man will be too embarrassed to go near this section of the market and will pretend he didn't see the item on the list.

10. Expect extra items. Men are very susceptible to advertising and cannot resist buying the product they saw advertised during the NBA finals.

11. Avoid putting "health food" items on your list. Men have a natural aversion to health food. If you mark down "eight-grain bread," they will buy white bread instead.

12. As your husband heads out the door, your final words should be "no replacements." If there is no fat-free yogurt on the shelf, he is not allowed to substitute it with Ben & Jerry's ice cream.

Finally, women, if you want to avoid disappointment, you need to lower your expectations. Realize that there is a 50 percent chance your husband will lose the shopping list on the way to the store and come home with junk food. Don't ask him to buy out of the ordinary things like "cumin." He doesn't even know what it is! Understand that even if he does the shopping according to your list, he will probably bag it wrong, putting the bread and eggs under the heavy pickle jars and beer six-packs. Give him a break. After all, he's only a man.

Pondering Packing

My wife and I went away for a long weekend recently. We took four bags with us. I had one small bag—an airline carry-on type—and in it I had:

1 pair of long pants
1 pair of shorts
3 pair of underwear
1 golf shirt
1 long-sleeve shirt
1 dress shirt
1 sweater
3 pairs of socks
1 toilet kit
1 paperback book

The other three bags were one large duffel bag, one stuffed hanging bag, and one large shoulder bag, all belonging to my wife. She brought:

3 pairs of long pants, one for every day we would be away
1 pair of blue jeans
3 shorts, to wear if the weather was warm
1 pair of silk pants, to wear out at night
2 skirts, to wear out at night
1 blouse to wear with the silk pants
2 blouses to go with the skirts
2 dresses, in case the skirts weren't fancy enough
1 sweater for daytime wear, fancy
1 sweater for hacking around, daytime
1 fleece pullover for daytime wear
1 sweater to go with the silk pants
2 sweaters to go with the skirt/blouse combinations

1 sweater to go with one of the dresses

1 shawl, to go with either the remaining dress or the silk pants

1 turtleneck

1 blue blazer, to replace any of the sweaters for nighttime wear

1 tweed sports coat, to go with two of the skirt outfits or the blue jeans

1 flannel shirt for daytime, if it got cold

1 heavy-cotton sweater, if the weather got cold

1 pair of shoes to go with the silk pants

1 pair of shoes to go with skirt set #1

6 pairs of shoes to match the other outfits

1 pair of sneakers

1 pair of flip-flops

1 pair of heavy boots, for walking

1 pair of shoes with heels and soles about twelve inches thick (This is "in"?)

12 different bras in assorted colors, to match assorted outfits

14 different types of underwear (see above)

10 pieces of miscellaneous other undergarments (slips, half slips, etc.)

1 long (to the floor) flannel nightgown (protection)

1 bathrobe

11 pairs of socks, for sneakers, boots, jeans, long pants, or just in case she needs more socks

2 pairs of stockings

12 pounds of assorted toiletries

5 pounds of assorted costume jewelry (to match the assorted outfits)

.005 pounds of real jewelry

1 winter coat, 1 summer coat, and 1 rain jacket

2 hats, one for day sports and one potentially for evening wear

2 pairs of gloves, one for day warmth and one for evening warmth

1 hair dryer (4 pounds—and they call it "portable"?)

1 travel iron (3 pounds)

3 hardcover books

8 magazines

2 catalogs

We had a lovely weekend, and neither of us ran out of clothes.

A Good Husband?

Over the years, I have observed many, many husbands and have come to develop a solid understanding of what makes a good one. Unfortunately, according to my lovely bride, I do not belong in the "good husband" category, and she is not sure I am even qualified to write on said topic. However, in keeping with the old expression "If you can't do it, write about it," here is:

HERB'S GUIDE TO BEHAVIOR THAT "GOOD HUSBANDS" OBSERVE

1. *Keep Your Trap Shut*: Every time a husband opens his mouth, he takes a risk. Good husbands are the strong *silent* types. They form many questions, answers, and comments in their minds but speak infrequently.

2. *Avoid Answering "No-win" Questions*: Good husbands realize that there are a number of questions with "no-win" answers. Innocently posed inquiries concerning weight, quality of food served, current attire, or hairstyles are actually male minefields where the truth, a fib, or partial truth can all be detected and lead to deteriorating relations.

3. *Pick Up Your Sneakers*: For some reason that I don't understand, most brides don't like tripping over sneakers left in the middle of the floor. This also applies to underwear and smelly, sweaty athletic gear dropped anywhere but the laundry room. Leaving beer cans or soda cans on tables, floors, and furniture is not behavior your wife will find endearing.

4. *Look But Do Not Comment*: If a man sees a cute young thing walking along the sidewalk, it is acceptable to glance casually, but he should not make any comments, gestures, or the like. Outright staring, ogling, whistling, turning around, etc., is prohibited, and even deep breath intakes are questionable. In general, if you want to be a "good husband," making comments about another woman's anatomy is to be avoided.

5. *Learn How She Likes Sweaters Folded*: According to my observations, women like to have closets, drawers, etc. kept in orderly fashion. The particular order and method is not uniform for all women but wife-specific. Learn the way she folds socks or stacks forks. Don't just stuff the sweater back in the closet any old way or put the pot back on any shelf. She only has to take it out and put it back "her way."

6. *Find Things*: I know you think that the mayo is not in the fridge, and your first reaction is to call your bride and tell her there is no mayo. However, the mayo is there—men just have a genetic defect that makes them unable to find it. To be a half-decent husband, you might look a second time, move things around, or do without.

7. *Avoid Pithy Comments*: I know you think you're a great jokester; however, your better half might not always appreciate your quips or comments. For example, when the package of new shoes arrives, don't say: "Hey, Imelda Marcos! Your ten-thousandth pair of shoes just arrived." Think these thoughts, but don't say them!

8. *Do the Honey Do List*: I realize you have plans to play tennis, watch football, or nap on the couch, but it is advisable to pay some attention to the list left for you on the kitchen counter. If she has to ask you three times to bring in the wood or she has to do it yourself, you will not be a candidate for Husband of the Year.

9. *Attempt to Fix Stuff*: She keeps you around because she thinks you are the strong masculine type and know things about cars, pipes, and electricity. So when something happens to the plumbing, don't just sit on the couch with the clicker and say: "Call the plumber." You should get up, take a wrench, and bang the pipes a few times, and then announce in an authoritative voice: "We need the plumber for this job."

10. *Don't Be Oblivious 100 Percent of the Time*: Yes, you have a lot going on (Super Bowl football pool, etc.), but you should try to notice when she changes hair color or rearranges the furniture in the living room.

11. *Empty Containers:* If you use the last of the milk, don't put the empty container back in the fridge. If you use the last piece of toilet paper,

replace the roll. If a woman discovers at the wrong time that there is no toilet paper, you could be a doghouse resident for an extended period. The same applies to paper towels.

12. *Remember Dates:* While anniversaries, birthdays, and Mother's Day might not seem like national holidays to a guy, they should be remembered in some fashion. If you really want to be in the "good" category (or get a free pass to play in the Saturday poker game), then a romantic gesture, such as flowers, is highly recommended.

13. *Write Down Messages:* If you answer the phone, get off the couch, find a piece of paper, and write down the message. It is not good form to tell her two days later, "Oh, someone called on Saturday about tennis. I'm trying to remember who it was."

14. *Be Alert for Subtle Signs:* Men prefer to have a woman tell him exactly—and clearly—what she is feeling and thinking, but women are more complex than that. You need to look for eyebrows raised, little sideways glances, periods of silence, and similar subtle signs that indicate things might not be perfect at the moment. If you miss the period of silence, you don't want to be around for the explosion that follows.

I realize that being a "good husband" seems to require a lot of work, but think about the alternative. Remember your bachelor days? Do you recall putting on dirty socks every day and eating off unwashed plates you took directly from the pile in the sink? Think back to the days when your diet consisted of pizza, takeout food, and burned chicken. Maybe following these guidelines and making an effort to be a good husband is worth it after all.

Keeping the Peace

The Happy Home Point System

Like most men, I live to keep my wife happy.

I've been struggling with this quest for over twenty-five years now, and I understand the game pretty well. Trust me, it is a game. You get points for being good and points taken away for being bad. So for the newlywed or anyone who doesn't understand the rules, here's an explanation of how points get awarded:

THE "KEEP HER HAPPY" POINT SYSTEM

You volunteer to go to the grocery store	+2
You forget half the things on the list	-1
You bring home large quantities of beer and snacks	-3
You take her out to dinner	+3
It's a Mexican restaurant, and she hates Mexican food	-4
You suggest a quiet romantic evening at home	+2
You fall asleep on the couch instantly	-2
You buy her flowers	+5
Because you forgot her birthday	-10
You buy her a present	+6
It is a home tool	-4
You buy her jewelry she doesn't return	+2
You buy her a slinky outfit from Victoria Secret	-4
She is dressed up, you say how pretty she looks	+2
You forget to say how pretty she looks	-10
You wait patiently while she tries on her 24th outfit	+5
You go sit in the car and beep the horn occasionally	-7
You say you will make dinner	+4
You serve microwave chicken fingers and hot dogs	-5
You declare you will do the dishes after dinner	+3
You do half the dishes and leave the kitchen messy	-2

You go to the video store for movies	+1
You bring home R- and X-rated movies	-3
You notice when she has a new hairdo	+3
You say pleasant things about the new look	+7
You miss the haircut despite numerous hints	-3
You go to her office holiday party	+5
You spend the entire time talking to a blonde	-3
You slow dance with the blonde (!!)	-25
You go to a social event and stay by her side	+3
You drink too much and demonstrate your singing skills	-3
You complete the "to-do" list she left you	+3
You sit around all day in your underwear and watch football	-5
You comment on how attractive her friend is	-5
You comment on how attractive and *skinny* her friend is	-12
You forget to write down phone messages	-4
You leave the toilet seat up	-2
You finish the toothpaste and don't tell her	-3
You leave beer cans around the house	-3
You forget to write down checks or cash withdrawals	-4
You don't praise her dinner	-3
You don't call and say you will be late	-4

Of course, you will notice there are many more negatives on this list than positives. That is a man's lot. It's an uphill struggle to keep our wives happy. Despite twenty-five years of trying hard, I am currently 6,785 in the negative column.

After the Hairdresser

A critical time in every marriage occurs when the lady of the house returns from the hairdresser. A man can be either a wonderful, loving husband or an insensitive cad, depending on how he responds to her new 'do. What he says will put him either in the great house or the doghouse, based on how carefully he chooses his words. Since I have visited both houses, I feel it would be beneficial to new husbands for me to pass on some advice about what to say when a woman returns from the hairdresser—or more important, what not to say.

• *Avoid sentences that end in a question*: This is a very sensitive time for a woman. She wants positive reinforcement, not questions like: "You paid $25 for that?" Or "Did you go to a new hair salon?"

• *Avoid jokes*: I know you are funny, but this is not a good time to test out your one-liners. She will not find the following questions amusing: "Did you go through a hurricane on your way home?" Or "Did you put your finger in an electrical socket?" Or "Is there a bird nesting in there somewhere?"

• *Do not comment on length*: If you say things such as "They took a lot off, didn't they?" You will draw this instant response: "I knew it was too short." Conversely, if you say, "They didn't take much off," she will think it wasn't cut enough.

• *Don't say things that imply big change*: For example, do not say: "It makes you look much younger." Or "It makes you look thinner," because she will automatically translate that into: "He thinks I look old" or "He thinks I look fat." You can't win.

• *Don't say things that imply no change*: At the same time, do not try to take the neutral road. The answer: "I can't tell the difference" won't cut it. She did not go to the hairdresser to hear you say that!

- *Avoid references to color*: When a woman does something to the color of her hair, that is something she does not want you to notice. Do not say: "Oh, you're a redhead now." Or "Where did that blonde hair come from?" Or worse, "That new shade of blue goes well with your eyes."

- *Avoid sarcasm or editorial comments*: If you stand back, tilt your head to one side, and say: "Is this the latest look?" you will not be popular. If you jump back in surprise and say: "I bet one of your workout partners talked you into trying that hairdo!" you will not win Outstanding Husband honors.

- *Don't forget to say Something!* A major faux pas guaranteed to land you in the doghouse is not saying anything. If you forget that she went to the hairdresser, and three days go by and you haven't commented on her new look, then you should be prepared for a prolonged cold spell.

What you should say: When your wife walks in the door, here are the words you should utter: "I love it, dear. It's perfect." If she asks you any of the above questions (Is it too short? Is it too long? etc.), DON'T GET TRAPPED! Don't answer. Simply continue to repeat: "I love it, dear. It's perfect."

Cold War

It's about time for the Cold War to break out again. I'm not talking about the political tension between Russia and the United States. I'm referring to something much more serious—the Cold War inside our house!

This war is fought because my wife thinks that forty degrees Fahrenheit is a comfortable temperature for a house and that a thermostat is a decorative item to be used only in case of an emergency. On the other hand, I am a normal person who thinks a house should be kept around sixty-eight to seventy degrees. Since the boss and I are about thirty degrees apart, the Cold War rages in our house from October to March.

Part of the battle will be verbal. I'll complain that the soup froze while I was moving it from the stove to the bowl and that the ice at the skating rink is warmer than our bathroom floor. Will I get sympathy? Will I get to turn up the thermostat? Of course not! She'll just say, "Put on another sweater."

I'll ask her why a man should have to wear a ski parka, gloves, and a hat to watch a football game in his own house. Or I'll ask if it's natural to see your breath while having coffee in the morning. She will say: "It's all in your imagination."

A lot of the Cold War involves the thermostat setting. When she is not looking, I try to sneak the setting up a notch or two, but instinctively, she senses it. "Boy, it's hot in here!" she'll say, "Who turned on the furnace?"

It becomes a little game. I move it up two degrees while she's at the supermarket. She moves it down three degrees while I'm unloading the car. I'll move it up to sixty-eight degrees while she's in Stamford shopping. She'll open several windows when she returns. It's a game I never win.

When I complain severely, she tells me to light a fire.

Unfortunately, a cold-blooded person like my wife must have designed the fireplace. It just teases a normal human like me. A good roaring fire is nice if you are sitting within six inches of it but beyond that distance, it is useless. I could cry thinking of all that good heat going up the chimney!

When we have a fire in the living room, the heat radiates just far enough to reach the thermostat for the ground floor. The temperature in the rest of the house drops to fifteen below zero, and I begin to feel frostbite in my fingertips. Then, if I stand right in front of the fire, my front side burns while the back half freezes. Believe me, a fireplace is useless for keeping a person warm.

Of course, the major Cold War battlefield is the bedroom. My wife likes what she calls "a little fresh air" at night. This means that she leaves the window next to the bed wide open. When I wake up on a winter morning, there is a snowdrift beside the bed, frost on the rug, and an icicle hanging from my nose!

You probably guessed by now that despite the Arctic temperature, she likes one thin cover over her, while I need an electric blanket, two comforters, wool sheets, and flannel pajamas. This results in considerable debate, boundary disputes, and cover protection. Unfortunately, what usually happens is that halfway through the night she rolls over and takes my layers with her.

While the international Cold War is now over, the Foster Cold War continues year after year. I complain that she's trying to force me to live outside where it's warm. She says having the house "a little chilly" is natural, healthy, and refreshing. I grant her the healthy part—no germ could live in the icebox temperature inside our house. And so it goes. It's really not fun to have an ongoing Cold War with your loved one. As a matter of fact, the whole situation leaves me cold!

The Nightmare of the Double Bed

My body is bruised all over. My back is aching. I have enormous bags under my eyes. Did I take on the New England Patriots single-handed? Have I been wrestling Magilla Gorilla? No, I spent two nights with my wife in a small, small bed. Actually, it felt as if I spent two years in that bed—or was it two decades?

You see, we went away for the weekend to a friend's house and got assigned to a small room on the third floor. In the middle of the guest room was an old lumpy bed, maybe four feet across. The hosts called it a double bed, but it looked like a doll's bed to me.

Now, in the sixteen years of what used to be a happy marriage, I never knew my wife to be a violent person. When I took the vows to love, honor, and balance her checkbook, I never suspected that she enjoyed inflicting pain on another. But then, of course, I can't remember ever sleeping in such a small bed with her. At home, we share a football field of a king-size bed. She has her side, and I have mine. I know that because whenever I feel affectionate and start crawling toward the other side, I hear a sound like a guard dog growling, and I know I have crossed the border.

The first evening in this tiny bed, I hit the hay a little early. I was almost asleep when I heard rustling sounds, and then felt a shooting pain in my lower back. I did some exploring and discovered—holy mackerel!—it was her knees digging into me! I never realized she had such bony knees.

When I politely suggested that she move, she shifted around until, suddenly, I felt a sharp pain in the back of my neck. Now it was her elbow. It was like a knife sticking me, hard and sharp. How come I never noticed that her elbows were actual weapons?

Again, I politely requested that she move over, only to be told not so politely that she was at the edge of the bed. I, too, was at the very edge of my side. We were beginning to see the difficulty of this situation. I finally asked if she would consider rolling over and pointing her sharp elbows and knees in the other direction. With some muttering, she agreed. I had a brief moment of pain-free existence, and then she curled up in a ball. In the process, she stuck out her back end with such force that I shot out of the bed like I had been thrown by a catapult. I landed on the hard wood floor with a thump. Oh, what fun!

These border skirmishes went on all night. I like to sleep with my head on my arm, but the hand sticking out went right in her face, so I tried to sleep in another position. I was just getting comfortable when she rolled over and the mattress adjusted, rolling me right into the center of the bed into a tangle of thrashing arms, elbows, and knees.

These "double bed" battles continued nonstop. Every move was aggravating to the other person and met with a counteroffensive. When you are in confines that close, even breathing is loud and offensive. At one point, she must have fallen asleep. I was lying there, sleepless, thinking of moving to the car, when she shifted her weight and her right arm came flopping over and hit me with a solid right cross. A sucker punch! For a second, I thought I was in the ring with Mike Tyson. Shortly thereafter, she kneed me in the crotch. I couldn't believe it. My own wife had turned into a dirty fighter!

The final indignity swiftly followed. There I was, lying there with a knifelike elbow in my side and bleeding from the nose, when she rolled over and took with her every last inch of bed cover. Not only the comforter but the blanket and all the sheets! It was bad enough that she was trying to beat me to a pulp, but now she wanted to freeze me to death!

It seemed as if each night lasted about a hundred hours. The two nights we were there felt like the equivalent of the Hundred Year War. When we got home after the weekend, the kids asked their mother why Dad was acting weird. "He looks like he's been mugged. He's twitching all over the place, and he's on his knees in the bedroom kissing the king-size bed!"

The FIP Policy

A few years ago, I instituted the Foster Important Paper (FIP) policy. It was one of the smartest things I have ever done.

This policy is simple: I, as a male, should not be trusted with any documents of value. No mortgage papers. No insurance papers. No deeds, liens, or liabilities. Nothing with seals or notary stamps and nothing on heavy parchment paper for me.

You see, being of the male gender means that I would put any of these items in a pile somewhere and forget where I placed them. When the important paper was needed, I would shuffle through piles, look in file folders, and mumble to myself that I was confidant I put it in a file marked "Docs." When I couldn't find it after a prolonged search, I would then accuse my bride of having removed it from the file. "Are you sure you didn't take it?" I'd ask.

Everyone knows that a man can't find the mustard in the refrigerator or a clean pair of socks in a drawer full of clean socks, so why should he be trusted with something as important as a deed? Everyone knows that a man thinks the Yankee schedule is much more important than the town tax bill, so why let him get his hands on the tax bill anyway?

I realize my friends are going to accuse me of being a wimp, of not wearing the pants in the family. While both of these statements might be true, I ask them to consider the rationale and benefits of the FIP policy before they condemn me.

This policy establishes clear responsibilities, so there is no more arguing. No statements like, "You were the last person who had it." Or "You took it out of the file when the renewal form came in." No finger-pointing or accusations.

Think about it. Splitting up these duties makes no sense. In a corporation, would the boss say to two people: "We want you both to keep half of the important documents?" No, of course not! They would put one person in charge. I just followed the corporate model and established a chief executive of important papers: my wife!

I felt the benefits of the FIP policy just recently. We were buying a new car and decided to trade in the old junk heap against the purchase price. Giving us our checklist, the salesman said, "I'll need the original title, and…" Instantly, I saw the panic in my wife's eyes. She would look for the document in the safe deposit box or maybe in her desk drawer, but she knew there was one place she couldn't look—at me!

Lately, I've modified the FIP policy to the AI policy—which stands for "Anything Important." Now, when someone calls and asks us to dinner, I reply: "Unfortunately, I don't have the authority to schedule dinner appointments. I am not reliable. You need to talk to the chief executive. Can I have her call you?"

Actually, I have expanded the concept to the ID policy as well, which stands for "Important Dates." The FIP boss is responsible for keeping track of relatives' birthdays, anniversaries, etc., and taking appropriate action (telling me what to do). This includes the FIP CEO herself. Her duties include reminding me when our anniversary is coming up.

Now, I realize my detractors will call me a sexist pig, accuse me of abdicating all responsibility, and dumping too much stuff on my bride. But you have to understand that in our normal division of duties, my bride has agreed to be FIP CEO. In return, she allows me to grill dinners outdoors eleven out of twelve months a year. So, before you brand me with your labels, ask yourself this: Would you rather have a husband who cooks many meals on the grill, or a husband who can find the car title? Or put another way: Would you rather have a husband who doesn't cook and still can't find the car title?

And besides, we have just followed a standard business practice—we have put the best person in charge of the job. My wife is organized, orderly, efficient, and smart. I'm just a guy who can't find the mustard.

Marital Communications 101

Every time I see a pretty young bride walk down the aisle, I can't help but think how little she really knows about marital communications. Specifically, no one —not her mother, the minister, or any married friend— has warned her that husbands come with substantial information-processing and communications baggage.

This young lady made it through the romance and dating stage—the time period when men actually listen, pay attention, and even attempt to express emotions. However, as soon as the honeymoon is over, a new communications phase begins. Or rather, I should say, a lack-of-communications phase begins.

As a service to new brides everywhere, I am going to give you a crash course in marital communications, right here, right now!

To start, here is a multiple-choice question for any woman who has been married for more than a year: You are standing in front of your husband, telling him something important. He is looking at you and appears to be listening. Which of the following things is actually happening?

A) He is thinking about what time the baseball game comes on TV and who is pitching.

B) He is making a mental note that he needs to go to the golf store to buy a dozen balls before his round on Saturday.

C) He is looking at you and wondering when you might feel romantic again.

D) He is actually listening.

Well, of course, the last choice is impossible. Ladies, you'll win the lottery before D happens.

Now, I know the men out there are saying: "There goes Herb

again. He's exaggerating. There are no communications problems." At the same time, I can see the wives are nodding their heads and agreeing. They have been fighting this battle since their wedding day: they know how difficult it is to communicate with him.

For those of you in doubt, see if these examples sound familiar:

A couple is riding along in a car. The man is driving and listening to the radio when his wife says: "The Smiths have invited us for a cookout on Saturday. Want to go?" The man grunts and nods his head, but on Saturday, when he is reminded that the barbecue at the Smiths starts at 6 p.m., he acts surprised. "When did we discuss going to the Smiths? I never said I would go. Do I have to dress up?"

Another example: A couple stops at a gas station to get directions, and the man looks directly at the attendant while he gives detailed instructions. A newlywed bride would sit quietly, not take notes, and drive off thinking her husband knows where he is going. Oh, what a mistake. A veteran of male communications wars understands that her husband only partially listened and has, at best, a vague, general idea of where he is headed. One turn and he is lost.

Some male issues not only involve listening (or not listening, as is the actual case) but also speaking. Husbands are very good at nonverbal communications: grunts, head tilts, hand waves, and, of course, shoulder shrugs. A wife asks her mate: "Did you have fun at the office party?" He makes a face and shrugs his shoulder. "Was that sexy assistant there again this year?" Husband's response: another shoulder shrug. (Is that man not a master of communications?)

Men also have difficulty expressing emotions. He might be angry about something, but when you ask if anything is wrong, he will say, "I'm fine." His jaw might be clenched, and his arm may be twitching, but all you will get out of him is, "I'm fine." Also, don't expect him to be overwhelmingly effusive in declaring his love on a regular basis, or expressing appreciation for all you do for him, or telling you how beautiful you are. Why? Because that's the way husbands are. (OK, not all!) Many men have learned the value of being the strong silent type (or in my case, the weak, potbellied silent type). They have been burned by answering questions about sexy assistants at the office party, about whether the outfit makes you look heavy, or if the new hairdo makes you look younger or older. They have learned that keeping the mouth shut has many benefits (except, of course, when they are in bed, asleep—then, they make plenty of noise).

This does not only apply to verbal communications. Men are not great with written communications either. Don't expect to have your husband write down phone messages, or write thank-you notes, or leave little love notes on the kitchen counter. (The note will more likely say: "no milk.")

So, here is my advice to newlywed brides:

1. Don't try to talk to your husband before he goes to work. He is rushed and thinking about all the work he needs to get done.

2. Don't call him at work. That is office time, and he doesn't want to be bothered with a question about the Smiths' dinner party.

3. Don't try to talk to your husband after he comes home from work. He is tired, grumpy, and just wants to relax.

4. Don't bother him on the weekend. That is his time to relax.

5. Don't talk to him when he is watching sports on TV. Heck, don't talk to him anytime he is watching TV.

6. Don't talk to him when he is doing the crossword puzzle, reading a book, or balancing the checkbook.

7. Don't talk to him...

Well, I guess I don't need to go on. Newlywed brides, I think by now, understand the challenge they are facing. But don't despair. There is an upside. After you have been married for a few years, you'll learn to take advantage of these male communications issues. You will go into the TV room during the final moments of a playoff game and ask if it is OK to invite the in-laws to spend a week or buy a new dress or whatever else you want. He'll agree to anything.

And in this modern world, there is one sure way to communicate with your husband. If he is home, in another room, or halfway around the globe, you can always get a response from him: Send him an e-mail.

Are You Listening?

Most people are not good listeners. They spend a great deal of time participating in conversations but not a lot of time actually listening. They are thinking about something else ("What a great shot I hit on the fourth hole!") or looking somewhere else ("I think I know that person") or are simply not interested ("Hearing about baby's toilet habits, I could do without"). They nod their heads and pretend they are listening, but their minds are not picking up what's going into their ears.

Because I have extensive experience with people not listening to me (I must be fascinating!), I have learned to classify the various types of nonlisteners into certain groups. They are the:

Looking Elsewhere Listeners: All the time you are talking to these people, they don't look at you. Their eyes roam around the room or look up to the sky. Sometimes you move laterally to get into these people's field of vision, but you only make eye contact for a fraction of a second, and then they flit away, looking anywhere but at you. You never have any idea if they are listening or not.

"On a Different Planet" Listeners: These people are the worst nonlisteners, the most aggravating people to talk to. When you say "I thought Bush did well in the debate," they reply, "I just bought a new car." They did not hear a word you said, and they don't even acknowledge your subject. Their response is on a completely new topic. After you talk with these individuals for a while, you're thinking: "Beam me up, Scotty. There's no intelligent life down here."

The Interrupters: These individuals won't let you finish a sentence or a thought. You start a sentence, "I was driving down 684 the other day, and....", and they jump in: "Isn't 684 terrible?" You actually weren't even going to talk about 684, but this type can't wait for you to finish. It's impossible to have a cohesive conversation with these interrupters because they do not really listen for the sake of good conversation—they are merely looking for an opportunity to interrupt!

"I'm More Important" Listeners: These people have to be better than you on anything you say. If you tell them about a new golf course you played, they don't ask you about the course, they tell you about one they played that's even better. If you tell them you saw a celebrity, they tell you about the time they had their picture taken with a celebrity. The entire time you're talking to them, they are not thinking about you or your experience. They are figuring out a way to prove they are more important or better than you. I call it one-upsmanship listening.

Challengers: These people can't leave well enough alone. They ask you questions about everything you say. They challenge your facts or they say things like, "I don't believe that." A conversation with these individuals is like a boxing match. They are not actually listening. They are simply looking for pieces of information that they can challenge or attack.

Part-time Listeners: These listen to about a third of what you say. They assume that they can pick up key words and carry on a meaningful conversation. If you are telling a story about your son struggling with algebra and French at school and how expensive part-time tutoring is, they say something like, "I had trouble with algebra, too." They don't mention your son or focus on what you were actually saying.

Intellectual Listeners: These individuals like only deep, intellectual conversations. They don't want to talk about sports or local activities. They want to talk about the meaning of life. Even at the lightest social engagement, they want talk about late-term abortions or the decline in morality among our teenagers. If you say anything superficial, they tune out. My advice to this group: Lighten up!

"Only Hear What I Want To" Listeners: Despite whatever you are actually saying, these listeners hear what they want to hear. You can say that the weather is partly sunny with a chance of rain, and these listeners hear that it is sunny. They pick one word out of multiple sentences, or one sentence out of multiple paragraphs, and that is all they hear. Their ears and mind filter information to suit their needs.

Sometimes when I encounter these types of individuals, I feel like reaching out and shaking them. They might be looking at me and nodding their heads, but I see that glazed look in their eyes. They appear to be listening, but they are on the fourth hole, or looking for a spot to interrupt, or waiting to steer the conversation back to their topics. I want to grab this person by the lapels, and say, "ARE YOU LISTENING TO ME?" I could ask this question, but why bother? They're not listening!

Asleep at the Meal

I am not a great dinner-party guest. I don't mean to discourage invitations, but when the name Herbert Foster comes up for consideration, don't think: lively, fun, interesting.

Why? Well, to start, most dinner parties don't even get going until around my normal bedtime. I am a morning person. I get up at 5 or 6 a.m. every day, and my brain goes dull (duller than normal, that is) after 9 p.m. My average conversation after 9 p.m. is usually "Huh?" or "Duh" or something equally stimulating.

Second, people always seem to schedule dinner parties on nights when I have had a very exhausting day. I drag myself home, and all I want to do is collapse on the couch and go to bed early. But no, my beautiful wife greets me at the door with the words: "Hurry up and get changed. We're late for the Jacksons'." (Sometimes this requires putting on a stiff-collared shirt, a jacket, and even a tie—further restricting the limited blood flow to my brain).

The dinner party normally starts with a cocktail hour. If my mind isn't dull enough to start with, all I need is a couple of cocktails to put me in a comatose state. Now, in addition to my smart riposte of "Huh?" and "Duh," I begin to drool from the corner of my mouth.

Then it's on to the dinner table itself. Under normal circumstances, I can stay awake at night if I am up and about and active. Unfortunately, dinner parties require me to sit in one chair for several hours. My body tells my brain: "We are not moving. Go to sleep." My eyes start to droop, and my head goes south toward the soup bowl.

I always feel sorry for my dinner-party companions because I am just not a great conversationalist. I'm not deeply versed in international affairs and have very little to contribute to a discussion on the economic challenges of the mid-European block. I'm not wildly interested in politics, and I avoid participating in the debate on the evils of the Bush administration's environmental plan for Alaska. Basically, I'm not well-read, unless you count the sports pages or comics.

What I am good at is saying the wrong thing at the wrong time. Just when the entire dinner table takes a pause and quiet descends, I say: "Did you hear about the scandal? Three hot chicks got sent home from school for wearing provocative clothes?" The quiet then continues at the table until one of the other guests says, "Yes. We heard. One of the girls is my daughter." Good job, Foster.

And as hard as my wife trains me, my table manners and etiquette remain questionable. From across the table, my wife will try to send me subtle signals to take my elbow off the table or to wipe the meat sauce off my chin, but all it does is draw everyone's attention to the spaghetti on my tie. Don't give me multiple choices of silverware because I am guaranteed to pick the wrong piece.

Then, of course, there's the ultimate disaster. I spill the gravy down the front of my shirt. Usually, this is a big, greasy stain, and the hostess insists on getting soda water and a towel. Just to call further attention to my clumsiness and lack of social graces, and despite the attention and fuss, the stain does not come off and I am marked for the rest of the party: inept dodo bird.

By the end of the evening, I can't wait to escape, but the hostess wants to serve coffee in the living room. This is the final torture. I am put in a soft, comfortable chair, somewhat like a bed. I am full of food and alcohol, and it's only a few hours before I normally wake up. If I even think about resting my head on the back of the chair, I'll fall asleep.

Then comes the very awkward time common to all dinner parties. It's when all the guests want to leave, but no one wants to be the first. Everyone knows that as soon as one person stands up, everyone will spring to his or her feet and sprint for the door. To avoid this, no one stands up, and everyone continues to try to maintain polite conversation.

Of course, my wife has an excuse to leave early—me! The polite conversation everyone is trying to maintain is difficult to hear over my snoring. She usually requires the help of a male dinner guest (or the local ambulance corps) to get me out of my chair, into the car, and home into my real bed. Not a pretty sight, but don't say I never warned you. I am just not a good dinner-party guest.

Reading Her Mind

Men, if you want to have a happy marriage, you must be able to read a woman's mind. Why? Because sometimes, when a woman says something, there's a hidden meaning behind her words. If you're going to be happy long-term, you need to be able to determine what the woman is really thinking and uncover the true meaning of what she is saying.

For example, when a woman asks, "Are you listening to me?" she doesn't mean, "Are you listening?" What she really means is: "I know you're not listening. I'm saying something important. Pay attention."

See, for a man to survive, he must be able to read between the lines, look behind the words, and determine the real intention. I'm hoping the following translations will help many a man, and create more happy households.

She says: "Do you think we need new curtains in the living room?"
She means: "I think the living room needs new curtains and maybe a new rug. It really should be totally redone. I was thinking of calling a decorator tomorrow."

She says: "I'm not upset."
She means: "I am so upset I am thinking of hitting you over the head with this vase. How could you be so dense?"

She says: "Do you love me?"
She means: "I did something today you are not going to like."

She says: "Do you REALLY love me?"
She means: "I am about to ask for something very expensive."

She says: "Have I told you recently what a wonderful husband you are?"
She means: "I'm about to ask you to do something you won't want to do."

She says: "If you want to do it, go ahead."

She means: "If you do it, I will make you pay for the next week or more."

She says: "It's your decision."
She means: "If you won't do it my way, then I wash my hands of it. Good luck, fella."

She says: "I'm going to look in the fridge and throw together some leftovers for dinner tonight."
She means: "I would like you to take me out to dinner tonight."

She says: "We need to talk."
She means: "You are in trouble."

She says: "I may be wrong, but..."
She means: "I'm 100 percent confident that I'm right. Don't even think of challenging me."

She says: "I don't care what you do."
She means: "I hope you don't care what you get for dinner for the next month."

She says: "Are you feeling strong?"
She means: "I have a piano I need you to carry up three flights of stairs."

And, of course, the ultimate is: "LOOK AT ME when I am talking."

This means: "I am really, really mad, and you're just sitting there like a lump. Stop acting like a caveman!"

Of course, there is another side to this story: What men really mean when they communicate with their spouses. But that's another story.

Suburban Struggles

The Dreaded Tag Sale

The tag sale is a great American institution. I know that. What I don't understand is why.

What is it about a tag sale that makes Americans willing to work for fifty hours to earn $43.25? Why are people willing to hurt their backs, strain family relations, and aggravate the neighbors for a profit of $22.40? It just doesn't make sense, but every week you see new signs on every tree and telephone pole in the county.

Let me describe my one experience with a tag sale as an example. My one and only experience—believe me.

We decided to do a joint tag sale with three neighbors. We picked a big field at the end of the street for the event. All week long before the sale, I make trips to and from the attic. I get home from work, change into old clothes, and start carrying. I have to work bent over double in the attic and then carry each load down two flights of stairs.

Say I drag down a box weighing fifty pounds. My wife inspects it. Among the contents are girls' white ice skates. We have two boys (how did those skates get into our attic?), but they can't be sold: "Cindy's kids will fit in those in a few years." Deep in the box is a cigar humidor (another mystery item: I have never seen it, and I don't smoke cigars), but this is not for sale either: "Grandpa would roll in his grave if I sold that."

As a result, I carry back up the stairs a thirty-pound box and then start down with another fifty-pound load. Up and down, all week long. By Friday, my back aches so much I am bent over like a pretzel, but everything is down from the attic. Since I am bent over to perfect table height, my wife rests a drink on my back, and says, "Time to do pricing."

What follows is a heavyweight championship bout—a full fifteen rounds. What is an old record player worth? No one can figure out if it works, and no one is willing to take the time to find out. Twenty dollars? No, too low. The ten-year-old decides he wants it. No. The record player ends up being thirty-five dollars, *as is*. The "as is" is important. No guarantees. It takes an entire night of negotiating to set prices.

Saturday morning I had to get up at 4 a.m. First, the signs had to go up. The whole time I'm attaching cardboard to stop signs and telephone poles, I'm waiting for the police to arrest me for defacing public property.

Then, starting at 7 a.m., guess what? It's back up to my favorite job: carrying boxes. Two hours loading into the car and unloading in the field. By 9 a.m., I have tears streaming down my face from back pain, and I smell like a gymnasium.

The sale starts promptly at 9 a.m. The neighbors are there with all their treasures. Everything is set, except there are no buyers. We wait. The sun beats down, and it gets hot. There are a few cars, but most people walk by our valuables at a brisk pace.

Around 3 p.m., we're getting worried. A man stops and looks at the record player, then says, "It's a big risk, but I'll give you five bucks." Now, five bucks sounds pretty good to me, but before I can say a word, my wife says, "Fifteen dollars." The man shakes his head and walks off. I want to cry out for him to come back. Heck, I'll pay him to take the thing away.

Around three-thirty, when our total sales come to $14, I get the worst blow of all. Bored, my wife wanders off, then comes back to borrow $10. She returns a minute later with a punch bowl and glasses, purchased from the neighbors! In the hundred years we have been married, we have never needed a punch bowl, and I can't foresee any occasion when we will ever use one. Not only that, but she just spent all the profits from the tag sale, plus $10 out of my pocket. We are in the negative column!

At 4 p.m. (the sale ends at five), we're getting desperate. Almost all offers are accepted—fifty cents for a $5 table; twenty-five cents for two unmatched ski boots. Unfortunately, our closeout sale started too late, so when 5 p.m. rolls around, there is still an enormous collection of unclaimed treasures.

A brilliant idea hits me. "Bonfire!" I tell my wife, "We'll gather around and have marshmallows."

"Not funny," she replies. "Start loading."

So, it's back to my favorite job—carrying boxes. Everything had to go up to the attic again, except for the record player, which the ten-year-old got in the end (it didn't work). The load that was the heaviest was the new punch-bowl set, which by the way, has never been down from the attic since.

The profits from our tag sale were $45.25, minus $24 for a punch-bowl set, for a net profit of $21.25. After two months I was able to stand up straight, and our neighbors are just beginning to talk to us again. I know I'm being un-American, but the tag sale will never become a tradition in the Foster family.

The 11th Commandment

In addition to the original Ten Commandments, there is an Eleventh Commandment in suburban towns: Thou Shall Not Covet Thy Neighbor's Babysitter.

Indeed, in these communities where houses sell for astronomical sums, a good babysitter is worth her (his) weight in gold, silver, and frankincense (Chanel scents, too). Women are trapped in their twenty-room mansions because they can't find a babysitter so they can go out on Friday night. Housewives are forced to postpone their shopping spree to the mall because they can't find anybody to watch Junior spit out his food or meet little Annie at the bus.

Wealth to women with young children is not measured by Mercedes station wagons or swimming pools but by child care. A woman who has a long list of available sitters (or a live-in) is wealthy beyond words and admired by all her friends. By this standard, a woman who can get a sitter for New Year's Eve is Ivana Trump to her friends!

As a result, women tend to become possessive about babysitters. They feel that if they use the same sitter on a regular basis, they develop usage rights. If they use the same babysitter every Saturday night, the person becomes "my sitter" and is therefore protected by the Eleventh Commandment. At the very least, they develop rights of first refusal every week.

They also gain special privileges if they "discover" a sitter. When the Joneses moved to town with a fourteen-year-old daughter, Mrs. Smith called the first night to welcome them and became the proud owner of a new babysitter. Like a prospector striking gold on unstaked land, she was thrilled by her find but couldn't tell a soul until she developed usage rights.

Unfortunately, once a woman finds a good sitter, she doesn't think to reserve that person for every Friday and Saturday night for the balance of her life. Babysitters themselves have no loyalty—they just want to make a few bucks. There is simply no structure built into the system. Believe me, it would be mass havoc—a housewife brawl—if it wasn't for the Eleventh Commandment.

While many women respect the unspoken rules governing babysitters, these are mostly women with available sitters. A mother without a sitter is more inclined to do something desperate. Women who would never think of stealing a candy bar will go to great lengths and develop all sorts of devious schemes to get the names of their best friend's sitters.

As a result, the most common crime in these suburban towns is not robbery or vandalism, it's babysitter theft. But this is not a crime that can be reported to the police. There are no official laws on the books, just the Eleventh Commandment.

Here's how the typical crime comes to pass: Two women are chatting over coffee, and one says "John and I are going to the theater Wednesday, and we're going to spend the night in the city!"

Her friend replies, "Oh, who did you get to babysit?" Note that she doesn't ask what play they will see or where they will eat dinner. She gets to the heart of the matter immediately. A sitter that can spend the night during the week is valuable.

With this question, the first woman's fur goes up. She pauses before replying, and finally says, "Oh, let me see. Who did I get?" She's being coy, but she's thinking, "There's no way she's going to get the name of this sitter." Of course, what she doesn't know is that her "friend" will telephone on the evening in question, and when she discovers (surprise!) that the parents are in New York, she'll say, "Oh, who's this? Oh, yes. Don't you live on Broad Street?" She'll get the name in the end.

About two weeks later, the husband will be met at the door by an irate wife, saying, "Guess who's babysitting at the Joneses' on Saturday night?" When he looks confused, she will continue, "Some friend I have. She stole my babysitter. She should have at least called me. I'll never talk to her again."

While the husband might be perplexed by this outbreak, every mother knows the severity of the crime this woman committed. She broke the Eleventh Commandment.

Be Our Guest!

The following guidelines are printed as a public service. My advice is to clip them out and mail them to anyone who might want to spend time at your house. They should also be posted prominently on your refrigerator, as a reminder.

INSTRUCTIONS FOR HOUSEGUESTS

We have a two-night maximum in our abode. We understand that you may find our guest room comfortable and the food excellent, but after two nights, you should hit the road. (Note: We may sound very disappointed that you are leaving and ask you to stay longer. We don't mean it. We are being polite. Pack your bags.)

We love pets. That is why we have three dogs of our own. I know your little Fido is an angel, but we prefer that the mutt not accompany you during your visit. Actually, strike the word "prefer"—four-legged creatures are simply not welcome.

We would like to put the same restrictions on children under the age of six but realize that might be a little rude. Therefore, if you insist on bringing your little ones, please remember that our youngest child left home several years ago. Our house is not childproof, we have no diapers, and, in our old age, tolerance is slipping.

Regarding children of older ages: If your visiting horde includes offspring between the ages of twelve and seventeen, please don't try to excuse their behavior as "just being teenagers." We don't buy that malarkey, and we will ask them forcefully to take their feet off the furniture. If your freeloading crowd includes little darlings over the age of twenty-one, tell them to bring their own beer.

We go to bed at 10 p.m. If you are coming to party hardy into the wee hours, expect that we will give you directions to Jimmy's Pub, the Wild One Bar & Grill, and other establishments that stay open to

2 a.m. Please don't wake us when you come in.

Ditto for those of you who wake up at 4 or 5 a.m. Don't get up and start banging around the house looking for the cream dispenser. Stay in bed until some civilized hour. When you hear one of us banging around looking for the cream dispenser, you may arise.

If you have dietary mandates, please tell us in advance. We don't know that little Jimmy drinks only lactose-free milk unless you tell us, and if you tell us at 9 p.m. on Saturday night when you arrive, we will be happy to give you directions to ShopRite or the Food Emporium.

Yes, we do have telephones. We have them so we can receive and make calls. If you want to use the phone, please use your credit card, and be brief. Very brief. Or perhaps your cell phone will work in our area?

Our computers are important to us. We know that you might want to check your e-mail, and we know you could make small "adjustments" to our systems to make them process faster. Unfortunately, you won't have the chance. We are not going to let you within twenty feet of our PCs. If you want to check your e-mail, bring your own laptop.

No. You may not "borrow" one of our cars. No way. No how. Don't ask.

Regarding houseguest presents: Wine is good (red—Cab or Chianti—if you must know). Do not bring anything that resembles a wedding present (tray, bowl, pitcher, etc.). We have plenty of those. Do not bring fudge or anything fattening. Do not bring kitchen utensils. Wine is good.

We, the owners of this abode, understand that some of these "guidelines" might seem harsh. However, please take into consideration the tariff you are paying for room and board before you take offense at the rules of the house.

The Guy Next Door

When my new neighbor moved in, I had no idea what trouble he would be.

He seemed very pleasant and friendly. He had a nice wife and child. I had no idea that he'd turn out to be a diabolical soul, bent on destroying the peace and tranquility we'd established on the street.

Up to this point, I'd really had no problems with the neighbors—except for little things like our dog stealing food off kitchen tables and our cat sleeping on the neighbor's bed. Nothing serious.

Looking back, I realize I should have foreseen the problem in the first few weeks, when he started working on his place with a passion—clearing brush, painting, washing, sweeping. I just assumed it was new-house mania and that it would go away in a few years. The problem, as you might have guessed, is that it didn't go away.

My neighbor gets up before dawn every Saturday and works until midnight Sunday. He doesn't pay golf. He doesn't play tennis. He barely stops to eat. As a result, his backyard is always immaculate. It's in perfect condition: the showpiece of Westchester County.

This causes several difficulties—for me, not him! The first is the obvious comparison of our side-by-side places. People love to make comments like: "Did you lose your garden tools?" "Having trouble keeping up with all the work?"

The truth is that my place isn't all that bad. It looks like a majority of houses in Westchester. It's just in the wrong neighborhood. It's next to *his* house.

To give you an example, let's talk about leaves. All fall, my neighbor rakes leaves every day. Barely has a leaf touched the ground when he has raked it up. My style, on the other hand, is somewhat different. I let all the leaves accumulate on the ground until the trees are bare and then rake once. It is really a much easier way of doing it, but for a three-month period, my lawn looks rather shabby in comparison with the pristine lawn next door.

A big part of the problem is that we have a set of picture windows that look right out toward his house. How can I sleep on the couch, drink beer, and enjoy a football game when I can see leaves flying, trees falling, and a tractor zipping about? I keep thinking it must be illegal or something. It's certainly un-American to work outside when a football game is on TV.

Or imagine this scene: I'm lying on the couch Saturday morning, reading the paper, when my wife the real-estate agent asks what I'm going to do that day. I tell her I have a busy day planned: finish reading the paper, go over to the golf course to donate a dozen balls to the tree gods, and then back to the couch to watch sports and take a nap. She looks out the window. I think she's staring wistfully off, until I realize that she's watching the neighbor clear brush. Is she wishing for a husband with no potbelly and a desire to rake leaves?

Now, I have tried several solutions to my problem. I have told the neighbor that his place looks so perfect that he doesn't need to touch it again, but he didn't bite. I have invited him to play tennis or golf, but he's not interested. Several times, under the cover of darkness, I've left a six-pack of beer on his front steps, but even that doesn't slow him down.

I'm now down to my last strategy, and I hope it works. Next week, I have a surveyor coming in to check our boundary lines. I'm going to try to convince him that my lawn is on his property!

Car-dinal Rules

Have you ever wondered if you've kept a car too long? How do you finally decide it's time to give up on the old jalopy and get a new vehicle? Well, here are some hints:

YOU KNOW YOU SHOULD GET A CAR WHEN...

1. Every time you pull away from a parking space, you leave a large brown spot on the ground.

2. You slam the door, and a flurry of rust flakes falls to the ground.

3. Driving with the windows closed, you can feel the wind in your face.

4. The neighborhood sixteen-year-old offers you $100 for it—and worse, you consider his offer!

5. Driving along the highway, you have to yell to make yourself heard by the other passengers.

6. You realize that the bumper stickers on the back are playing a major role in keeping the car together.

7. The automatic car wash refuses to let your car go through because they are afraid it will fall apart in the process.

8. The tow-truck driver says something like, "Oh, you again?"

9. As you get into the car, you always sit down gingerly because you're afraid the seat will fall through to the ground.

10. A potential passenger decides he would rather walk than ride in the car.

11. Your garage mechanic brags, "I sure know that car pretty well. I've worked on every inch of it, inside and out."

12. You can tell how fast you're going by looking at the ground move under your feet.

13. Your entire trunk is filled with things like jumper cables, wate bottles, screwdrivers, and flares.

14. Your repair shop puts your car in their Frequent Failure program.

15. Your insurance agent asks that you find someone else to insure the car.

16. You cross yourself and say a few prayers before turning the key to start the car in the morning.

17. Someone asks when you are going to apply for "antique" plates.

18. You have to use string or a bungee cord to keep your trunk closed.

19. Things labeled "automatic" are no longer automatic.

20. You're too embarrassed to park in the office parking lot, so you park next door and walk.

21. A 5 percent incline represents a major obstacle for the car.

22. Your teenager no longer asks to borrow the car.

23. You don't care if the radio doesn't work because you can't hear it over the car noise anyway.

24. You need to know a special trick to get the car started. If you don't know the technique, you can't get the car to run.

25. Your car is too old to be listed in the Blue Book of used-car prices.

26. You avoid driving in cities because you're afraid you will break down in a busy intersection.

27. The election bumper sticker on the fender says "Goldwater" or "McGovern."

28. The neighbors ask if you would mind not parking the car in your driveway, because it's bringing down the value of homes in the neighborhood.

29. You're driving with the pedal to the floor, and cars behind you are honking their horns.

30. You start weighing luggage or any cargo before putting it in the trunk.

31. You figure out that your tires are worth more than the car itself.

32. And of course, the ultimate signal that you need a new vehicle is when you go to take the dog for a ride, and the dog refuses to get in the car!

Report Card on Maddy's First Birthday

Dear Well-Known Dog Breeder:

Thank you very much for the one-year birthday card you sent for the female black Labrador, Maddy, you sold my wife. She really appreciated your card. In the spirit of a one-year anniversary, I thought it might be appropriate for me to give you a "State of the Union" address. Here is my report:

The dog you sold us is a terror. A sock-eating, mess-creating terror. A one-dog demolition team. A tail-wagging house wrecker. A sharp-toothed, wanton wild woman. She is like the rest of the women in my life: smart, aggressive, determined to have her way, and, of course, she refuses to listen to me or obey me at all.

I have stopped counting the number of items that Maddy has destroyed, but the list ranges from many small items like hats and gloves to slightly larger items like my barbecue grill and wheelbarrow. I write this letter today wearing a pair of old eyeglasses. Why? You-know-who destroyed my expensive new prescription glasses.

This mutt has razor-sharp teeth that can cut through any surface. NASA has yet to discover a metal that Maddy can't mutilate easily. She has annihilated "guaranteed dog-destruction-proof" toys in less than thirty minutes. Unfortunately, a large percentage of the items she obliterates give her diarrhea in the middle of the night.

To date, the dog has been through four screen doors. The first two were normal screen doors, but the third and fourth were reinforced with heavy-duty screening, which proved to be only a minor obstacle for our little puppy. We have now replaced all screen doors with half-inch-thick steel grid, which we hope will last through next month.

In the past, when it was cold or raining, we would leave the garage door open a little, and the dogs would sleep inside on dog beds, protected from the elements. Unfortunately, this does not work with Maddy, who has decided that whenever the garage door is open, her mission is to empty the garage into the driveway. Rakes, shovels, the lawnmower (she is strong enough to move almost anything) end up spread around the landscape. The last time she did this, I was surprised the neighbors didn't think we were having a tag sale!

Maddy might have a great career in redistribution or "clutter creation." If I spend a Sunday picking up twigs and making the yard immaculate, the next day, when I return from work, the lawn looks as if a tornado has hit! Maddy has done the following: taken a dozen pieces of wood from the woodpile and spread them around the lawn; removed the cover and tools from the grill and left them in the front walk; pulled down the deer fencing around the flower garden, spread the poles over the landscape, and chewed ten plastic flowerpots into a million pieces; and, of course, when I arrive, she is sitting there, looking sweet and innocent, tail wagging.

We also have a small problem with getting packages delivered with Maddy around. The overnight companies leave deliveries on the front porch. Maddy looks at these with an expression of great enjoyment that says: "Oh, look, someone left me a toy." Within minutes, the cardboard box is in a million pieces, spread around the front yard, along with its contents.

But worst of it all is our sock problem. Maddy has a fascination for socks and constantly wanders around with a sock in her mouth. We cannot leave a sock on the floor, in the laundry basket, or anywhere Maddy can reach, or it's good-bye sock. By my informal count, I believe she has destroyed 432 pairs of socks. She is also quite fond of wandering around with underwear in her mouth. This can be slightly embarrassing when we have guests.

There is no question that Maddy is smart. I say this because she was housebroken in just a few days, and then got a master's degree in people walking patterns. While our other Lab does his duty as far away from the house as possible, Maddy lays her little jewels in a perfect land-mine pattern, making it impossible to take even a few steps outside without hearing that telltale squishing sound underfoot.

The most irritating part of this whole situation is that I have totally fallen in love with the dog. To watch her rollick through mud puddles is pure joy. When she comes and puts her head on my knee, looking for a scratch behind the ears, I think she is the cutest, most adorable dog I've ever seen. That's the upside. The downside comes when I get up the next morning and can't find my socks, can't open the screen door because it has twenty pounds of steel fastened to it, and then step on something smelly and squishy on the lawn. I know she's just a one-year-old, but how long will I have to live with missing socks?

Sincerely,

Herb

Small and Friendly Is Best!

I am a "small town" type of guy. What does "small town" mean? To me, it's not determined by population or acreage or geographic location. It's people, neighbors, a feeling of friendliness. A "small town" could actually be a neighborhood in a bigger city or a very little rural village. It's…well, maybe you should take this "small town" quiz to see what I mean.

When you walk into the gym in the morning, you:
a. see no one you know.
b. recognize several faces but don't know their names.
c. see your minister, your insurance agent, and several good friends.

When you see a police car coming toward you, you:
a. immediately slow down and look in the other direction.
b. drive carefully as you can and avoid eye contact.
c. lower your window and yell out: "Hi, Joey! How's Wendy?"

When you see a dog hanging around outside the deli, you:
a. complain to the deli owner.
b. call the police to notify the dog warden.
c. call Paul and Joanie, and tell them that Barkus has gotten out again.

When you see a car stopped by the side of the road, you:
a. honk at them for getting in your way.
b. drive by quickly, looking straight ahead, scared of trouble.
c. you stop, roll down your window, and ask if you can help.

When you need a new pair of shoes, you select a store:
a. because you can save $3.50 on the price.
b. because you saw an ad in the newspaper.
c. because you have always gone to that department store, you know everyone there, and to go anywhere else would be disloyal.

When you see a sign for "Ham Night" at the firehouse, you:

a. decide to avoid that section of town that evening.

b. go in the hopes you might win a ham or another prize.

c. go because you will see all your friends, and you like supporting the volunteer fire department.

When you get to the grocery store and realize that you have forgotten your money, you:

a. turn around, and go home.

b. go to the ATM machine.

c. tell Joe, the store owner, that you'll pay him the next time you come in.

When you lose your purse at a charity function:

a. you never see the purse again.

b. you get it back when the organization finds it and mails it to you.

c. Susy recognizes the purse as yours and gives it to Julie, because she knows you two play tennis every Tuesday and Thursday.

When you call a wrong number, the person you reach:

a. hangs up on you.

b. says: "Sorry, wrong number.

c. recognizes your voice, says hello, and gives you the correct number of the person you were trying to call.

Needless to say, I want to live in a town where C is the correct answer to all the questions. When I go to the post office, I want Earl behind the counter to say, "Hi, Herb!" I like being able to pull into a parking lot and know who is there because I recognize their cars. I guess what I am saying is that I'm just your basic small-town guy.

A Letter from the Labs

Dear Mr. & Mrs. Foster (or can we call you Mom & Dad?):

The two of us Labrador retrievers have been living with you for several years now, and while we are generally happy with our existence, we do have a few items we would like to discuss with you.

To start, can we clear up the guard-dog/pet thing? As we understand it, you want us to be friendly and nice to everyone except burglars. You want us to greet Tony the mailman, the UPS guy, and family visitors (whom we don't know) with a wag of the tail, but scare away bad guys? Can you explain to us, simple little dogs, how we are supposed to tell the difference? Do bad guys come with bright red name tags or something? Here's your choice: either we growl and bark at everyone, or we give all visitors the tail-wag-and-welcome-lick routine (we are currently working in the latter mode, and think that is more fun).

We have the same dilemma when it comes to barking. You want us to bark to drive away deer and the aforementioned bad guys, but not at nighttime. Isn't that when deer and bad guys normally arrive? You want us to provide an "early warning system," but not bark when you have guests or whenever you want quiet. The thing is, in case you missed it, we haven't learned to speak English or dial 911, so how are we supposed to differentiate? Barking is the only thing we know. It's what we're supposed to do.

Also, we'd like to clarify the command thing. We understand what you're trying to get us to do. You have yelled "Come!" about a thousand times. We are not dumb; we know you want us to come. However, you must understand that we have priorities. For example, we may be sniffing a delightful smell off a tree (from Mrs. Smith's beautiful setter). After we have done the sniff routine, we need to add our pee to the collection around the tree. Then we will be obedient and come running (unless we encounter another aromatic tree on the way back).

But not before.

Just remember the old cartoon from *The New Yorker* with two dogs talking. One says to the other: "I know more commands than I obey." It is true with us, too. When you say "Sit," we know what you mean, we just need to figure out why you want us to sit, how important it is to you, and what other options we have.

So, while we are doing this human-performance appraisal, let us list a few other complaints we have:

When you take us for a walk on leashes, you pull us away every time we get to an enchanting odor. These pee smells on telephone poles are dog communications—you're not even giving us enough time to read our mail!

And let's talk food. Do you eat the same food every day? Of course not. So why do you force us to eat the same dry dog food day after day? A little variety would be nice, thank you.

We should discuss the "smelly" thing, too. You accuse us of being stinky when we come back from a walk or swim in the river. Just between us, we love that odor; it's how dogs are supposed to smell. And by the way, we don't love all that perfume and aftershave you wear, so we are even.

I know you think a pat on the head and the words "good dog" are suitable reward for a member of the canine species. However, given our choice, we would prefer something more tangible, like a steak bone. Oh, heck, just give us the steak.

And how about treating us with respect? Don't make us wear those stupid bows and bells at Christmas, or wear a collar that says "Vicious Guard Dog."

In essence, you have to get over the fact that we are not human. We do things dogs are supposed to do. We scratch, we lick our privates, we stick our noses in places you wouldn't, and yes, we shed. Don't grumble about us leaving dog hair everywhere. It's not as if we have a lot of control over it.

And here's our final complaint: You know, don't you, that there are two things we love: to be scratched around the ears and to have the ball thrown for us? We could do these things for hours and hours, but you only do it for a few minutes now and then. We're willing to bark at the deer/strangers, respond to your commands, and all that stuff, but you have to pick up the ear-scratching/ball-throwing time substantially. Deal?

Yours Ever Faithfully,
Maddy & Murphy

Handy, I'm Not

My Big Red Toolbox

I have this big red metal box that I keep in the laundry room. My wife thinks it contains implements of destruction. I call it my toolbox.

The box contains all the equipment I like to use to fix problems around the house. However, when my wife and kids see me coming with it, they put in earplugs and run for the hills. I don't know why, because inside this box are many useful items, such as:

A HAMMER: I use this to put dents in the wall near the nail I'm trying to hit. I also frequently use this device to enlarge my thumb and force me to utter expressions that explain my family's need for earplugs. This tool also has a reverse side that allows me to remove the occasional nail that I actually strike and bend over double. I use this reverse side to further damage the area I'm working on, before inserting a new nail and starting to hammer the walls and my fingers again.

SCREWDRIVERS: I use these items to ruin the slots on the ends of screws so it is impossible to get them to go in 100 percent. I usually get the screw to about a quarter inch from the surface when the head of the screw becomes an unrecognizable mess and I lose all patience. At this point, I am both unable to finish the job or remove the screw, and I am forced to turn to more aggressive measures. To complete the project, I usually opt for the back end of the hammer, as I mentioned above, or if it's really stuck good, my sledgehammer never fails to do the trick.

PLIERS: I use these items, similar to the screwdrivers, to round off the heads of bolts and injure my wrists. I have never actually found a pair of pliers that was the right size or seemed suitable at all for the job at hand; therefore, I'm convinced the key to using these tools effectively requires more power and less technique.

NEEDLE-NOSE PLIERS: These are very handy for removing splinters and retrieving bolts dropped under the washing machine. I am not sure what other use they might have.

POWER SAW: I usually balance the wood I want to cut on top of a garbage pail and use this tool to throw the wood back into my stomach, inflicting substantial pain and, again, forcing the issuance of expressions of displeasure. I always seem to underestimate the RPMs this machine can generate until I see the wood flying at me.

JIGSAW: I use this item for cutting uneven, erratic patterns in wood. When I am finished using a jigsaw, the wood I have cut looks like it has been cut by a slalom skier , zig-zagging down the surface, totally ignoring the straight pencil line down the middle of the board.

TAPE MEASURE: I use this for roughly estimating distances and dimensions. I have never found this to be a reliable tool, and despite my skill with it, anytime I have used it to measure and cut two pieces of wood to be the same length, I have found the end results to vary by at least an inch. A picture hung with this tool is never centered on the wall.

PAINTBRUSHES: I understand that these should be used to apply liquid of some type, but since they weren't cleaned properly before being put back in the red box, the brushes are as soft as cement. I therefore use these for hammering nails when I have mislaid the hammer.

SCREWS, NUTS, AND BOLTS: Although there are approximately two thousand screws lying at the bottom of my big red box, none of them is the size I need. Ninety percent of the time spent on a project is taken up rummaging around the box looking for a screw of the right size. The same applies to nuts and bolts. Although the box contains every imaginable size of nut and bolt, it is impossible to find two that match in size and will fit where they are needed.

INCOMPLETE TOOLS: My red box contains eight hacksaw blades but no hacksaw. (I occasionally try to use these without the handle, with interesting results.) There is also an electric screwdriver with no bit and miscellaneous other tools that are missing essential parts.

UNIDENTIFIABLE TOOLS: Also in my red box is a collection of implements that came with the original set, but I have no clue what they are for. There are little metal things with beveled edges, wood things with sharp edges, and a bunch of plastic things, too. I don't want to throw them out because I'm sure they're useful for something—I just have no idea what for.

I don't have the space here to review all the contents of the box. There are old batteries, fuses, pencils with no lead, empty matchbooks, and hundreds of other items. My red metal box is full of all sorts of useful equipment, and I have no idea why my wife starts calling repairmen when she sees me coming with it. I like my red metal toolbox!

Easy Does It!

I have just finished putting together an "easy-to-assemble" computer table and have decided that I want to meet the guy who wrote the instructions. He is probably the same one who wrote the manual that came with the bike we bought last Christmas, or the little cards that come with license-renewal forms. This guy is the Ernest Hemingway of assembly writers—he's world-class all the way.

He provides you with a long list of parts, labeled from A to JJ, accompanied by a drawing of each. However, when you open the box, the drawings bear no resemblance to anything inside. There are eight sizes of screws, numbers 1 to 7a in the instructions, but only four sizes in the kit. The smallest screw in the drawing clearly has a round head, but the smallest screw you find has a flat head.

The instructions tell you to spread all parts out on the floor. They don't tell you that you need a room as big as a football field to do so. You carefully work your way through the assembly, number by number, until you come to #10, which starts off "Now, before the glue dries on #9 (of course, you, following directions, waited patiently for the glue to dry before proceeding on)…" Stage 13 calls for four washers, but search as you might, you can find only two.

Now, I ask you—how difficult can it be to write clear directions? How hard would it be to label a piece of wood AA so you know immediately what it is, instead of thinking it was BB and gluing three things to it. How difficult would it be to write instructions that make sense? The answer is obvious.

Therefore, I have come to the conclusion that they make assembly instructions confusing on purpose. I have a mental image of the guy who wrote the manual sitting around with a bunch of coworkers laughing like crazy as they write the brochure. I hear conversations like this: "Hey, Joe. What if we get them to hold this with the left hand, hold this with the right hand, and then have to screw in this bolt? Get it? It can only be done with three hands!" Then they all fall to the floor, laughing hysterically.

Or "Let's take these two side panels, put three holes in one, and two in the other, and then provide only four screws! They'll never figure it out!" The group is now howling and slapping each other on the back.

For fun, they visit the man packing the boxes: "Give this guy two extra dowels. That'll confuse him."

Or "Let's throw a wrench in this box that doesn't fit anything!"

They probably have a covert union (UAW—United Assembly Writers) and exchange trade secrets. For example, tip #10: "Use self-locking screws, so when the assembler makes a mistake, he can't correct it."

The union hands out awards every year to writers for instructions that are virtually impossible to follow: "Our top award goes to John Smith, who wrote the brochure for a bicycle. When you assemble it according to his instructions, it is impossible to get the wheels to turn. Great job, John!"

This union might even get secret payments from other trade organizations. For example, plumbers of America pay royalties to the man who wrote the instructions for the "Easy to Install Icemaker Kit." When anyone less than a master plumber tries to use this kit, they are guaranteed to break a pipe, get wet, and have to pay the plumber $200.

Maybe there is even a college where writers learn a special vocabulary and artists learn how to draw eight sizes of screws to look identical. Whatever, there is one thing we know for certain: the people who reach the top of this profession automatically get recruited for the highest honor. They begin writing income-tax forms for the IRS!

I Am the Pain in Painter

Whenever I use any home-repair tool, my wife is scared. But when I pick up a paintbrush, she gets really afraid.

Usually when I'm working on something broken around the house, I'm just delaying the call to a professional who will come fix the problem. Yes, occasionally I make the situation worse, and yes, I almost always make a much more extensive mess than would any home-repair professional.

Not so with the paintbrush! With this tool, I can inflict permanent damage or, at a bare minimum, make some painting company very rich. What might start as a little "touch-up" job to be done on one windowsill gets out of control when the paint starts getting splattered around and can easily lead to an entire room being painted!

I have decided that my lack of painting skills is not only a question of manual dexterity (I have none) or hand-eye coordination (ditto), but a question of patience, too. I have less patience than a roadrunner, and you can see it in my painting.

It starts with the prep work. I sand and scrape until the wall looks totally ready to me, but when I paint, there are more bumps, hills, and canyons than you'll see in Yellowstone Park. After I put on the first coat, you can see the poor prep work from miles away.

Then, when I finally get down to the real job, I have a small problem with distribution. I get more paint on the floor, on my pants, and my hands than I do on the surface being painted. No rug within fifty yards is safe when I have a paintbrush in my hands. For this reason, if I am painting a wall, and the paint shop says it will take one gallon, I order two. I know that at least 50 percent of what I'm attempting to apply will end up someplace other than where it is supposed to be. And it's easy to tell what room I'm painting in. Just follow the trail of drops from the garage!

And again, my poor prep work comes into play. I was too lazy to put down a complete cover for the floor and furniture. I thought a couple pieces of newspaper were enough. Little did I know it would look like the "white-paint tornado" had come through after I finished.

My least favorite surface to work on is the ceiling. If I'm painting the ceiling white, every inch of my body and the floor gets coated with white paint, but I get very little on the ceiling. When I'm done, people are easily confused as to whether I was actually painting the floor or the ceiling.

Painting a windowsill and sashes is no picnic either. It doesn't matter how much tape I use or how fine a brush, when I'm done the window is opaque. Then I have to scrape the window with razor blades, ruining my new paint job in the process.

And I've never been able to handle a rag. I have seen professional painters hold a rag in one hand, so that if a drop goes astray, they lightly touch it, and it disappears. Not so for Herbert. When I touch with the rag, I smear the surface, hit new areas, and create three new problems, all worse than the original.

Then comes cleanup time. If I paint for one hour, it takes at least three hours to clean up after me. First, all the surfaces that got paint but weren't supposed to be painted have to be cleaned. Then I'll attempt to remove paint from my clothes (it's usually just better to throw them out), and finally, there is extensive work needed on my body, hair, nails, and shoes.

This is why my wife takes vehement exception whenever I pick up a paintbrush. She humors me when I take out a pair of pliers or a wrench and lets me play with them a while. But when I pick up a paintbrush, she is very firm. She comes over immediately, pats me on the hand, and takes it away from me, saying: "Let me have that, dear. You're not allowed to play with those. Give it to Mommy."

Black Thumb

I am the exact opposite of those folks who have a "green thumb" and whose plants or vegetables grow beautifully. You see, I have a black thumb. It does not even have the slightest hint of green around the edges. Almost everything I plant goes to the great garden in the sky before its time.

I have a large vegetable plot. It is in an excellent location. It gets full sun. It has good drainage. It has an eight-foot-high fence around it to keep away the dreadful deer. It has good soil. There is no logical reason to explain my horticultural shortcomings. No rational explanation. Just a bunch of sorry-looking plants, all wishing they had been adopted by someone with gardening skill.

My wife grows flowers in the same garden space, and they do beautifully. (Both her thumbs are green.) In the same soil, I can't even grow zucchini. Have you ever heard of a vegetable gardener who can't grow zucchini? Neither have I. It's pitiful.

I don't know why I fail. I start with strong, healthy plants. (After repeated failures, I gave up growing plants from seeds. Now I go to the nursery and get healthy seedlings. All the way home, I can hear them crying in the back of the car.) I work hard in my garden, but I must be doing something wrong. Am I overwatering, underwatering, overfertilizing, or underfertilizing? Maybe all of the above? I have no idea, but the results are the same. I try to kill insects and pests, but I murder the plants in the process. I should be arrested for what I do to my vegetables.

The one thing I can grow very well is weeds. You have to wonder why I can't make a plant sprout when the weeds flourish so nicely, but I can't explain it. I plant beet seeds, expecting to have to thin them as soon as they poke their heads above the soil, but by the time they pop up, there are so many weeds, I can't find the beets!

I grow squash, and it sends out long tentacles for yards around. The plants look healthy. Blossoms come, and I start warming up the stove for my first squash harvest, but as soon as the squash fruits begin to develop, a root borer gets the plant, and everything frizzles up and dies before I get one meal.

People give me tips, but they are no help. My stepmother told me to put out little saucers of beer to kill the slugs. (True!) As far as I can tell, not only did I not terminate any of the slimy fellas, but they seem to have acquired a taste for Budweiser and are very, very happy in my garden.

If you toured my garden, you would see a thriving, busy environment, unfortunately not thriving with plants and ripe vegetables but creepy crawly things. My plants attract more bugs than ripe Camembert cheese. I get slugs, cutworms, beetles, earwigs, maggots, cabbage worms, borers, aphids, caterpillars; you name it, and I've got it. Suffice it to say that if it eats vegetables or is generally bad, it lives in Herb's garden.

In addition to the bugs, my garden has frequent visitors from outside the fence, such as rabbits, woodchucks, skunks, and the like. I think the fence is tight, but the varmints get in. They take the lettuce and leave me droppings. And what they miss, the birds get from the sky!

The final produce from the garden is pathetic. My tomatoes look as if they have been through the Civil War. They have holes, large cracks, dark black spots, and, of course, little green worms. In a family that loves tomatoes, no one will eat mine. Sometimes my tomatoes go from green to mush overnight on the vine.

It's embarrassing. My cucumbers look like prunes. My cherry tomatoes look like raisins. My cauliflower is not white, my broccoli is not green, and my beets are not red. Frequently—read: 100 percent of the time—the leaves of my vegetables get multiple black spots and holes, turn a strange yellow-orange color, and crinkle up at the edges. When I take a sample to the garden store, the experts all shake their heads and say: "I've never seen *anything* like that. Never."

The ultimate irony is that I usually go away for two weeks in the summer, and what little produce manages to survive my ineptitude and poor treatment matures during these two weeks. When I get back, everything has passed. The lady from my wife's office who stopped by tells me that she enjoyed the tomatoes, zucchini, cucumbers, and all the rest, but when I look in the garden, all these plants are dead, dead, dead.

In addition to my lack of skill, I have no luck. When I planted asparagus this year, I followed the instructions exactly, including digging two-foot-deep trenches. From the moment I planted those asparagus, it rained continuously, and my trenches became mini lap pools. Swimming on the surface were the lovely asparagus roots, or, I should say, the quickly rotting asparagus roots.

Fortunately, when a lot of rain comes, it is a big help to me. Now I am no longer the only person whose vegetable garden looks like a rugby field after a game. Almost everybody in town is growing the same crop as I am: mud. Yes, mud, mud, and more mud. Even those folks with the greenest of thumbs can't produce anything in this environment. I am on equal footing for once. Bring on the rain!

A Funny Thing Happened on the Way to the Wood Bin

I'd get all my odd jobs done easily if it weren't for the things I have to do before I begin the jobs.

On Saturday morning, when I checked in with the boss for my honey do list, she said there was only one thing she wanted me to do: fill the wood bin in the living room. I practically ran from the scene, thinking I'd gotten off easily. This job would only take a few minutes, and I'd be free.

However, when I walked around behind the garage, I discovered there were no split logs, and that I would have to chop some wood before filling the bin. No problem: I would get out the ax, and I'd still be done in no time.

When I opened the garage door to find the ax, I realized that it was fairly well buried behind a mess of tools and equipment. "While I'm looking for it," I thought, "maybe I should clean up the garage a little, kill two birds with one stone." So I started emptying out the garage onto the driveway.

As I pulled out the wheelbarrow, I noticed it had a flat tire. Since I knew it would be easier if I had the wheelbarrow to cart the wood after I split it, I began looking for the tools I needed to remove the wheel. In the process, I came across the chain saw and remembered that it needed to be sharpened, so I paused long enough to remove the chain and put it in my car to take to the repair shop. After all, I might need the chain saw during the wood-gathering process.

Finally I assembled the proper tools to get the wheel off, and did this, placing it in the car (next to the chain) for the trip downtown. Returning to my search for the ax, I came across a bunch of old cans that should go to the beverage store for recycling. I put those in the back of the car as well, thinking that I should also pick up some beer while I was out.

I ran the tractor for a while to make sure it was running properly, cleaned up an oil spot underneath it, and made a note to get oil while I was downtown. The last thing I found, before locating the ax, was a bicycle that my son had borrowed from a friend last summer but never returned. I cleaned it up and put it on the rack on the back of the car with the intention of stopping by the friend's house on the way to do the other errands.

When I finally found the ax, I noticed that the handle was slightly cracked. Thinking that this might be dangerous, I decided to get a new handle—I was going to the hardware store anyway—and change it before attacking the woodpile. It took some time to remove the old one, but after a while the ax went into the car with everything else.

All of this had taken longer than I had hoped, and it was near lunchtime before I was ready to head downtown. However, I was very organized.

I returned the bike, dropped off the saw chain, went to the gas station to fix the wheelbarrow tire, and then the hardware store to buy the new ax handle. I did the can-sorting thing at the beer store, bought some microbrewery samples, got the oil for the tractor, and then returned to pick up the chain before heading home. Of course, I had to talk to the proprietor at each establishment for a few minutes (a guy thing), get lunch, buy lottery tickets, get cash, and do a few other errands, so this outing took longer than anticipated.

Once I got home, I worked in reverse. I put the chain back on the saw and filled it with gas so it was ready to use. Then I put the tire back on the wheelbarrow and put the saw in the wheelbarrow. I was feeling good now. I was making progress. Putting the new handle on the ax took longer than anticipated—I had to get help from my neighbor and help him with a project in return—but finally, that job was done as well, and I even sharpened the ax for good measure.

The day was now getting on, and I realized that I should probably finish the garage-cleaning project before chopping the wood— the boss would not be happy if she returned to find the driveway covered with the contents of the garage. I finished taking everything out. In the back, I came across the birdseed, so I cleaned and filled the bird feeders; then I found the windshield-wiper fluid, so I filled the cars. I swept out the garage and carefully put everything back, hanging tools in their proper places, sorting the screwdrivers, etc. along the way. I was proud of the way the garage looked when I was done and felt I had really accomplished something.

Unfortunately, it was now near dark and too late to chop wood safely. I decided to leave the wheelbarrow, with the ax and saw in it, just inside the door, so I was ready to begin chopping first thing on Sunday morning. I thought I had had a productive day, but the honey-do master had a different opinion. She came home, took one look at the wood bin, and turned on me: "I only asked you to do one thing. One simple job. Was that too much to ask? What have you been doing all day?"

She stomped off before I could tell her about how productive I'd been, to tell her about the wheelbarrow, the chain saw, the garage, the bike, the beer, and everything else. She obviously has no appreciation for how long it takes to get organized and ready to begin preparing to start work on a project.

It's Old, It's Quaint, It's a Pain

We live in an old house. First-time visitors often say, "It's so quaint." Well, "quaint" to me means that the house, like its inhabitants, is showing its age.

An older house is nothing but trouble and expense. People talk about a boat being a hole into which you throw money. Well, an old house is worse. When I go visit someone in a new house, I am in awe. Everything works. Everything is level and shiny. There is no peeling paint, no shutters off-kilter, no lights that flicker.

Our house is the exact opposite. We have windows that can only be opened by an Olympic weightlifter. We have doors that won't close, period. They are so crooked that months of sanding wouldn't help. Our floors are so far from level that when you drop something round in the middle, it instantly rolls to a corner.

When you ask someone to come replace a broken cabinet door, they laugh. "They haven't made parts for those things in many years. You'll have to replace the whole thing." When electricians come and open the electrical box, they step back and grimace. You can tell by the expression, they are thinking, "I'm not sure I want to go in there."

It's like living in a museum. An expensive museum. Our windows still have counterbalance weights. The wooden shutters, the porcelain sinks, and the outside light fixtures are so ancient that they belong in an antique store. We have toilets that were invented before outhouses!

An old house is full of surprises, too. One day, for no reason at all, a piece of plumbing in the crawl space broke. The plumber suggested (of course) replacing all the piping under the house, but the quote he gave us was slightly more than the cost of a new Mercedes, so we went for the patch job, knowing it wouldn't be long before the same plumber was back, in the same crawl space, fixing another broken pipe.

When some workmen came to install a new ceiling in the kitchen, they asked us a very difficult question: Do you want it level or do you want it on the same plane as the floor? Our answer, naturally, was, "Which would look better?"

Have you ever tried to hang wallpaper in an old house? You start perfectly aligned to the right-hand wall. Your seams between pieces are perfect, but when you get to the left edge, the top fits snugly but there is a three-inch gap on the bottom because the walls aren't parallel! It's fun.

You would think that an old house would have completely settled. Not so. Replaster and paint a wall, and it will have cracks in it within a year. Redo a ceiling, and little paint flakes will start dropping within months.

Since I am not handy, all the repairmen love the fact that I have an old house. These people know our crawl space intimately (they have nicknames for all the mice that live there). I'm sure I am personally responsible for putting several workmen's children through college.

Of course, one of the big disadvantages of an old house is that it's impossible to keep clean. Visitors will admire the wide-board floors, but all my wife sees are the large cracks in between the boards where dust, dirt, and all sorts of things collect. You can imagine what it was like when the kids dropped their spaghetti and the sauce ran into the cracks.

If you buy a house built before 1900, you must understand Old House Rule #1, which is: The house will need repair faster than you can fix it. If you have the outside of the house painted, the living-room walls will start to peel. If you're forced to replace all the plumbing in one bathroom, the electric connection to the outside lights will stop working. You will be swimming against a rising tide of repair.

Of course, some of you are probably thinking: "If the Fosters' old house is so much trouble, why so they still live there?" Well, you know the answer. We're still in the same house because it's so quaint!

My Life, My Lists

I am a list maker. I make lists every day, for work, for personal things, for projects, for shopping. I carry pads, little cards, and even loose pieces of paper. I have so many lists that I need a list to keep track of all my lists!

When I get up in the morning, I make a list of all my work projects. Actually, I take my list from the previous day and rewrite it, item by item. Each work category has an underline, and underneath it are specific jobs to be done, all in three orderly columns on a large lined pad. It appears to be all-encompassing but is far from it.

This list covers all projects I'm working on, but does not specifically identify jobs that must be accomplished within the next twenty-four hours. So—you guessed it—I make another list. This is an offshoot of my big All Project list, and I call it my Day List. It only includes things I must get accomplished before I go beddy-bye that day.

For example, I might have "Prepare presentation for meeting" on my All Project grouping until the morning before the meeting, at which time it quickly goes on the Day List." Or "Write column" will hang out on the big list for a while, with no action, and then it makes a panic move to the Day List shortly before it is due.

To further complicate matters, I also use stars on my lists, especially the Day List, to indicate projects with high priority, things that need to get done immediately. Stars mean: you *have* to do this, it's due, people are waiting for it, you promised it would be done, etc. etc. Sometimes, when it's especially important (or late!), an item gets two stars.

These two lists are very helpful; however, most of the items included are work oriented, so, yes, I keep a separate list of personal projects to be done, things like: "Clean office," "Put away lawn furniture," "Get birdseed, and more. A number of the items on this particular list come from the office of the supreme commander and frequently come under the heading of Honey Dos.

This list is fairly long and contains a number of projects that are only there as window dressing (frequently projects requested by the chief operating officer mentioned above) and really are not under active consideration. For example, "clean garage" has been on this list for weeks (OK, years). It obviously needs to be done, but I don't have the time, energy, or ability to attack a project of that size, so it gets transferred from Honey Do list to Honey Do list. (These jobs exist in a kind of project purgatory, where it's possible they'll reside forever.)

To further organize myself, my personal list (and the others) get yellow-sticky sublists—Post-it notes with little mini "to do's." For example, if I am about to go out and do errands, I will take my lined pad with personal projects and attach a Post-it organizing my route: dry cleaners, post office, gas station, Harry's, Nick's, etc. etc. (There is nothing worse than fighting the traffic on Route 117, then realizing you forgot something and having to double back into the fray.) Of course, I sometimes use stars on the sticky notes as well.

But needless to say, I can't take my organization pads (work, personal, etc.) everywhere I go (the minister hates it when I write on my pad during his sermon), so I carry little white cards in my pocket to record things that come up when I am padless. If someone asks me to do something while at a social gathering, it goes onto a little white card.

I would like to say that this is the end of my lists, but it is not. Whenever my wife and I have a "meeting," the result is another list. We make lists of work we would like to do on the house (if we could afford it). We make lists of vacation spots we would like to visit (if we could afford it). We make lists of holiday presents we would like to get for the kids (if we could afford it). Etc.

I think you are getting a picture of my life; it's definitely not listless. I have all these pads with lists (All Projects, Day, Personal, House Improvements, etc.), and on the lists are stars, sometimes two stars, and on top of the lists (and stars) are yellow stickies with sublists (with stars), and next to them is a pile of white cards with other lists (sometimes with stars).

One challenge to the system is the appearance of not-listed

work. I have tried very hard to discourage people from giving me projects that don't reside on one of my lists. I think it is very rude when a client calls up and says: "I want you to do this," and the job is not on one of my pads—and especially doesn't have any stars! I tell them that my life is very well organized without their input, but for some strange reason people who are paying me to work for them don't understand this concept.

I have also discovered that about half of my day is consumed by items not on my project lists. There is no line item on the pad for "Answer phone calls," "Respond to e-mail," "Make lunch," "IM with buddy," etc. In addition, I have the attention span of a gnat (post-windshield), so as soon as someone sends me an e-mail that includes a joke or any reference to baseball, golf (heck, any sports), women, politics, the weather, etc., I drop everything I am doing to read and respond.

So if you see me wandering around town with multiple pads under my arm, with all the yellow Post-its and paper sticking out of every available pocket, understand that I might look like a mess, but it is just Herb's way of keeping organized, and I hope you appreciate what a major job it is for a list maker like me to amalgamate all the notes that reside on pads, Post-its, white cards, an occasional envelope, and toilet paper into true project lists that help keep my life in control. The question, of course, is: Am I spending too much time preparing the job lists and not enough time on the jobs themselves? I'm sure I could evaluate this, keeping track of my time by, naturally, starting another list.

No Decorating Genes

I know I get into trouble when I offer advice to women, but trouble or not, here goes. Ladies, please don't involve your man in an interior-decorating project.

I can hear the women now: "Here goes sexist-pig Foster again." But it's true. Most men are just not comfortable with color schemes, furniture placement, or curtain fabrics. The reason is easy to explain. Decorating is not in men's genes. Consider the evidence:

Men think "peach" is a fruit, not a color. They think burgundy is something you drink, not an appropriate tone for a sofa. They don't understand why someone would think cream and mushroom are drape hues.

Most men have no idea what a sideboard is and shouldn't be asked to comment on where to place one. For most men, "valence" is a guy who used to be in old Western movies, and "chintzy" means that somebody is cheap. For them, Chippendale refers to a male exotic dancer.

In addition, men and women have natural inbred differences with decorating. Men traditionally like dark green, deep red leather, and paneled wood. Women like pinks, pastels, patterns, and frilly frou-frou borders. There is no middle ground. Trying to put a pink frilly curtain over a red leather chair just doesn't work!

To men, comfort is the most important element. Women care most about how it looks. Men want functional. Women want appearance. Get the picture? We have irreconcilable differences here.

When a woman tells a man she wants to redecorate a room, his instant reaction is: "Why? What's wrong with what we have? It works fine." Men don't see tired fabrics, worn rugs, or out-of-style design. They think things are pretty comfortable the way they are.

Ask a man to decorate a room, and what you get will be a large-screen TV with a recliner chair, a couch to sleep on, and a small refrigerator for holding beverages. The color or fabric of these items is not important, as long as it is not frilly or pink and the man is allowed to spill occasionally on the furniture.

In consideration of his genetic predisposition, please, please, never ask a man to select "coordinates." Show him three different fabrics side by side, and his eyes gloss over. Show him fabric, wallpaper, and rug selections at the same time, and he will be totally paralyzed.

By and large, men do not have a natural appreciation for the finer points of decorating, like using antiques. Furniture is for sitting on, holding something, or putting your feet on, not for collecting. If a table is fragile or the surface important, don't put it close to where a man sits frequently.

When there is a major decorating project going on, there is only one thing a man cares about: price. When you ask a man what kind of fabric he wants on chairs, he will ask one question: What is the least expensive? He sees no need for the fancy trim around the windows if it costs an extra $1,000. The windows look fine plain, thank you.

Most men have finally come to the realization that the decorating process goes much smoother if you say "Yes, dear" frequently. Other good word choices are "I trust you judgment," and "Whatever you decide is fine with me, dear."

So, ladies, here is what you do. Go ahead with your decorating project. Tell the man what you are doing when he is watching TV or reading the paper. He will say, "Yes, dear." He will not be happy with all the details of the finished product (especially the cost), but the decorating job will be done with a minimum of aggravation for both of you. He won't understand why you wanted a duvet cover or even what a duvet cover is, but then, of course, you don't understand why he was upset when the Giants tried that draw play on third and eight. It's a man-woman thing. Trust me: if men were meant to decorate, they would have been born with decorating genes.

They're *Your* Kids

The End of an Era

Whitey passed away this week, and we buried him under a solid two inches of soil. His departure was a cause of grief for some in the family, and a great relief for others. At least he got a better burial than his brother (or was it sister?), Toby Two, whom we flushed down the toilet. When I threw the last shovelful of dirt on the grave, I knew we had competed an era in our family history. Every family has to go through a goldfish phase, and ours was now over.

This phase started out innocently enough at a fire-department carnival. When older brother departed to go on the Upside Down Cookie Thrower Ride, his younger brother asked for a few coins to try "the penny pitching game." I gave him six pennies, and off he went. Now, I really didn't think much about that exchange and was waiting patiently when I felt a tug at my sleeve. I turned around to find younger son holding a plastic bag with water and two goldfish inside! My mouth dropped open, and I was speechless. Finally, I was able to choke out the word "*No*."

Instantly, two big tears appeared on his cheeks.

"Wait," I said. "We have no place to keep him. We have no aquarium or any of the equipment."

Four more tears started down each cheek. No crying yet, just tears—a sure sign I had a difficult battle ahead. I put my arm around his shoulders and was about to start on the "fatherly" approach when his brother returned and saw the bag. "Neat-o," he said. "Can I have one?" The younger brother, quickly realizing the value of an ally, nodded his head. Immediately, I knew I was in trouble, and that the Foster family had acquired two goldfish.

After the bag leaked all over my car on the way home, and the fish spent the night in a large Hellmann's jar, we went off in the morning to get a proper home for the animals. After prolonged debate (the boys thought a tank the size of a small swimming pool was appropriate), we selected the $18.95 aquarium, plus $8.25 for a circulator, and $6.10 for food, white gravel, shrubbery, and artificial rocks. When I walked out, I was $33.10 lighter and really steamed at the fire department. Why can't they just give out teddy bears or yo-yos?

After doing interior decoration on the aquarium (does the rock look better on the left side or the right side?), we got the fish settled and named them Whitey and Toby. That first day, the two boys were constantly looking at the goldfish, and I discovered later, feeding them every half hour.

The next morning, I was awakened by a bawling child, who dragged me by the hand to the aquarium. There, I found Toby floating belly-up, probably dead from overeating (something I might die of, one day). Off we went to the pet store again, for "Toby Two"—or is it Toby Too?

We worked out a feeding schedule, and TT made it through the first night. We settled into a routine for about six months. The boys totally ignored the fish, and the real -estate agent and I were stuck with feeding them, paying someone to feed them when we went on vacation, and keeping the aquarium clean. Believe me, it is a constant battle trying to keep the sides of the bowl from turning green and the rocks from turning brown.

I thought the boys had totally forgotten about the fish until, one day, the youngest said, "Dad, the goldfish are getting flaky." Sure enough, both animals looked as if they were gathering bread crumbs, and a day later, Toby Two went to the great aquarium in the sky. Without realizing there was a moral issue involved, I gave TT an unceremonious send-off into the plumbing system.

I was reprimanded at the dinner table. TT was a member of the family and deserved a better departure. I didn't have long to wait to correct this, as Whitey passed away during the night. We went down into the field, dug a small hole to give old Whitey a proper burial with full ceremony and a grave marked with two sticks tied together.

Prior to the funeral, I had prepared all sorts of arguments on why we shouldn't go to the pet store and replace these creatures. I needn't have worried. After the ceremony, the boys went off to play ball, and I went to wash the aquarium and put it in the attic. I smiled as I did it, knowing that the goldfish era in the Foster family was over.

Camp Creature

Today, my son came home from camp.

Although I was waiting for his car pool to arrive, I first realized he was close when a distinct odor overtook the neighborhood. I was looking around for a garbage truck when the car pulled in. The passenger door opened, and a small brown and green thing jumped out, followed by a horde of flies! I was waiting for my son to get out when I realized the thing was running toward me with arms open.

I kissed at arm's length, stood back (it was impossible to breathe up close), and said, "Let me look at you." That was actually very difficult, because I really couldn't see much except brown and gray. I couldn't tell if he (it?) was simply tan or actually 100 percent solid dirt. I could just barely make out shorts, T-shirt, several Band-Aids, numerous cuts, and bruises.

"When was the last time you had a bath?" I asked.

"Dad, we went swimming in the lake every day," he said.

I wasn't sure if that was a clear answer, but in the meantime I had noticed that his teeth had a distinctly fuzzy look. I tried again.

"When was the last time you brushed your teeth?"

"Come on, Dad," he replied. "The counselors checked every day to see if the toothbrushes were wet." Another precise answer—you don't think they just stuck the toothbrushes under the faucet each night?

I didn't want to ask when or why his blond hair had turned black; I simply insisted that he take a prolonged bath before he sat on any furniture. Actually, if I had been thinking clearly, I would have taken him to the car wash. Our white tub has been brown ever since.

After two hours and four washings, what emerged was a fairly normal-looking boy, except for the long claws on each hand and foot. With a chain saw and hedge clippers, we were able to make these look like fingernails and toenails.

My wife and I stood back, proud of our work, when the camper said, "Oh, I brought you a present," and started for his duffel bag. We smiled until we realized where he was headed, then intercepted him quickly. Sitting in our front hall, looking innocent, was a bomb about to explode. We carried the bag gingerly into the middle of a large field, tied a string to the zipper, and standing well back, pulled gently. Sure enough, a large mushroom-shaped cloud appeared instantly.

We separated the clothes inside into three piles: 1) Beyond saving—to be burned; 2) Moving/possibly alive—to be buried; and 3) Undistinguishable, due to green fungi. After destroying piles 1 and 2, we took a hose to #3.

Now, you have to realize that one short month before, we had invested several hundred dollars in white and blue camp uniforms with hand-sewn name tags in each. What emerged from under the hose was a Bruce Springsteen shirt (name tag: "J. Hamlen"), two pairs of jams (no tags), eight baseball shirts, and three bracelets. Not a single item had his name on it.

The question-and-answer period that followed was as productive as the first session. "Where did all your camp clothes go?"
He shrugged his shoulders and said, "Oh, we traded a lot."

My wife said, "You have absolutely no underwear or socks! How can you live without underwear or socks?"

This time he smiled as he shrugged his shoulders. "Easy," he said.

All our questions drew the same one-word answers until I asked if he had had a good time. "Fantastic! Out of sight!" he said. "Can I go again next year?"

The "Do You Really Want to Have Kids?" Test

I saw an article on the Internet recently about how young parents should take a test to determine if they are ready to have kids. I agree wholeheartedly and have expanded the concept with a few thoughts of my own. Here are some test exercises that I think a couple should complete before having kids:

1. *House-Destruction Test:* Look at your nice clean living room. Take a Hershey bar and push it around (and into) the fabric of the sofa. Take crayons and draw on the white walls. Put a slice of pizza underneath the cushion of a chair. Put your favorite vase on the mantle and then nudge it with your finger until it falls on the floor and breaks into a million pieces.

2. *Sleep-Deprivation Test:* Go to bed at 10 p.m. Have your alarm clock go off at 10:47. Pick up a ten-pound weight, carry it around in your arms, and sing to it until 12:25. Put the weight down and go to bed. Have your alarm clock go off at 1:18, and repeat the singing to the weight procedure until 3:05. Go to bed, and set your alarm clock to go off at 4:22 for more weight singing. Repeat night after night.

3. *Shopping Test:* Borrow a monkey from the zoo. Go to the supermarket to do your normal shopping and try to keep the monkey from knocking down the Pepsi display, breaking catsup bottles on the floor, or stealing candy while you are trying to check out.

4. *Adult-Appliance Test:* Take your VCR and shove an Almond Crunch candy bar where the tapes normally go. Take your favorite CDs and, after throwing them around like Frisbees, use them as steps on the gravel driveway. Bend your stereo headsets so they can be used as a slingshot to shoot mud balls at the neighbor's kid.

5. *Continuous-Carrying Test:* Get a backpack. Fill it with stones and a

CD player that is continuously playing a loud, aggravating tape. Carry it around during all your waking hours, on your left hip, then right hip, then in arms, etc. Talk on the phone, clean the house, and more—all without putting the backpack down.

6. *New-Floor-Covering Test:* Get the following: jacks (those spiky things with small ball), pick-up sticks, two dozen carpet nails, marbles, and several ice-cream sandwiches. Now spread them around the floor of the TV room, turn off the lights, and walk around in your bare feet for several hours.

7. *Clothing Test:* Get six balloons, blow them up halfway, and cover them with baby oil. Attempt to put all six balloons inside one baby overall outfit, and just as you are about finished, pour water on the crotch of the outfit and start the process all over again. Repeat four to six times each day.

8. *Eating Test:* Make a bowl of oatmeal. Hang an empty quart-size plastic Coke bottle from the ceiling with bungee cords. When you have the bottle bouncing up and down, try to put spoonfuls of the cereal into the mouth of the bottle, while saying: "Here comes the train. Toot. Toot. Open the station doors." After you have failed repeatedly, knock the cereal bowl on the floor, spilling considerable quantities on your pants as you do.

9. *Trip Test:* Before going to the in-laws for dinner, spend two hours packing paraphernalia needed for the evening, including a car seat, stroller, mini crib, diaper bag, blankets, clothing change, etc.; one bag of food stuff, including bottle, formula, pabulum, utensils, baby food, etc.; a backpack with baby wipes, baby oil, powder, and more. Take an hour loading into the car (don't forget the baby) and an hour unloading (best done in the rain).

10. *Changing Test:* Using the blender, prepare a mixture of refried beans, curdled milk, sausage, and sardines. Put it out in the hot sun until it has gone bad and the odor can be smelled several miles away. Ten times a day, put this mixture into a cloth diaper, carry it

around for a while, then discard. Occasionally, sprinkle water on yourself while changing the mixture.

11. *Dress-for-Success Test:* Go to work every day with spit-up on your shoulder. Just before you leave to go to an important meeting with a client, take blueberry chewing gum and press it firmly into the front of your suit. Discover that the bows from your very expensive shoes have been removed and stapled onto the front of a paper airplane.

In general, plan on putting away all lengthy books with high intellectual content. Your primary reading material in the future will be about bears that climb trees. Instead of adult conversations, you should be prepared to spend your days making choo-choo, cooing, and animal sounds. Put away your long hours of lying on the sofa, listening to classical music, and being surrounded by peace and quiet. Instead, your new life will be filled with an ever-changing, constantly moving bundle of joy, fun, and love.

If you pass the tests, you are ready for the most wonderful and fulfilling experience a human can enjoy!

They'll Drive You Crazy!

Driving home on Labor Day, I passed a car and saw an individual with twitching lips, red face, and shaking hands. Immediately, I recognized the signs of a person traveling with young children.

Although my little ones have grown up and are driving themselves, I remember too well the pain, the torture, and the challenges of traveling with kids. Actually, given my extensive experience and knowledge in this area (spending many hours looking like the person described above), I thought I might pass on some tips for the uninitiated.

HELPFUL HINTS FOR DRIVING WITH CHILDREN

Don't assume that "car games" will hold a youngster's attention any longer than thirty seconds. Counting yellow cars or state license plates will amuse an eight-year-old for about a nanosecond. He or she will then return to doing something really aggravating, like hitting the dog with a seat belt.

DO NOT, under any circumstances, give chewing gum to a child in a car. It is very difficult to remove gum from seat fabric, carpeting, and the dog's fur. One stick of gum can do an unbelievable amount of damage.

Never let a young child go alone into a bathroom with an inside lock on the door. You will spend hours yelling at the door, "Johnny, unlock the door. Johnny, please turn the round knob." This also applies to car doors. Trust me. It is *very* embarrassing to stand next to your car in a rest area, begging your beautiful young one to unlock the car!

Don't think that headsets will allow the kid to listen to music and not bother you. Even with a headset on, the volume is so loud inside the car it can drive you to tears and draw complaints from other drivers.

Make the young ones go to the bathroom in a rest area, even

if they say they don't have to. They will tell you they are fine during the stopover, but will "desperately need to go" about three miles down the road. This also goes for food. They are not hungry when you are near a restaurant, but five minutes later they will be starved.

Ice-cream cones with two or three scoops are definitely a bad idea. The chances that one scoop (or the entire cone) will fall on your carpet is somewhere between 95 and 100 percent. Not only will the car get dirty, but the young one will make major noise for a new cone. Ditto for pizza. When pizza is dropped in a car, it automatically falls with the cheese-and-grease side down.

Do not believe that a "no-spill" lid on a container means it won't spill. Kids can make the tightest "leakproof" cup spew forth liquid like a garden hose.

Never give your kids medicine that is supposed to make them drowsy or sleepy. They will become wired and have more energy than a band of uncaged monkeys.

In fact, don't make any attempt to control their sleep patterns. Kids on the road will be awake and whine continuously when driving, but when you get to your destination, they will fall asleep and miss everything you made the drive for. It is beyond your control—they will fight all the way to the relative's house and then sleep while they are supposed to be meeting Aunt Julie and Uncle Bill.

DO NOT put on their "dress-up clothes" before the drive in the car. Clean, pressed clothes are an automatic magnet for dirt, grape juice, hamburger grease, spit-up, and worse. (Yes, there is worse.)

When a kid says, "I have an upset stomach," *believe him.* Don't say something passive like, "You'll feel better soon." Stop the car immediately and take action to prevent ruining the inside of your car.

Avoid, if possible, traveling with kids *and* dogs. The complications and distractions multiply exponentially. And of course, don't *ever* leave windows open with pets in the car, unless you don't have a problem with Fido jumping out on Interstate 95.

Know before you start that your offspring will get into a fight just when the driving becomes most difficult. When you reach the complicated intersection, the backseat occupants will start crying at the top of their lungs and begin banging their heads against the window.

And of course, never respond to the question: "How soon will we be there?" and all its permutations ("How much longer?" "Are we there yet?" etc.). Respond once, and these questions will be asked every fifteen seconds for the duration of the trip. Not only will you be driving, but also you will be driven crazy!

The First Apartment

My son, Charles, makes outstanding chicken parmigiana. He learned the basics from me and is really good at preparing this dish. That is the good news. The bad news is that this is the only thing he knows how to cook. He can probably boil an egg or open a can of SpaghettiOs, but that's about it.

This topic is relevant today because young Charles has now graduated from college and moved into his first apartment. For the last four years, he was eating school meals or fast food. While this young man has outstanding expertise with computers, stereos, and other electronic equipment, he suddenly was ushered into a world of mechanical devices that he knew nothing about: a stove, a dishwasher, a clothes washer, a dryer, and a vacuum cleaner. He was also unfamiliar with less mechanical items: pots, pans, bowls, a broom, a mop, a toilet brush.

Actually, Charles's first-apartment experience involved much more than just food and cleaning. When we picked him up at college, he loaded up two cars full of stuff, so you would think he had enough junk to fully equip an apartment. Not the case. Included was a trunk full of college souvenirs (shot glasses, bumper stickers, pictures from spring break, etc.), stereo equipment, a dartboard, hundreds of CDs, several tons of laundry, and other possessions essential for college life. Apart from the stereo equipment, there was very little that could help furnish a new apartment. There were a few sheets and blankets but most of these had only been washed once or twice in four years. These were quickly declared unsalvageable by Mrs. Foster and discarded.

One of the larger transitions for Charles was taking responsibility for his own laundry. For the past four years, his method of doing laundry was to let everything accumulate until Thanksgiving or Christmas or some other occasion that allowed him to stuff it all in a large bag and bring it home for Mom to wash. Unfortunately, now that he was out on his own, that method would no longer work.

The biggest challenge facing this young man was to furnish and equip his first apartment. The initial thing he did was what people in his position have done for years and years: he ran his own private scavenger hunt in the Foster house. He found an old bureau and a bed in the back of the attic, a very dilapidated desk in the basement, and an old fan in the garage. He took everything he thought would be remotely useful, including a bread maker (which I am willing to bet a thousand to one that he will never use). He then finished off his furniture shopping by buying a sofa for $5 from someone about to throw it out.

The next thing he did was also traditional: he played on the heartstrings and natural maternal instincts of his mother. With an innocent expression, he asked a simple question like: "How do I make coffee in the morning, and what do I serve it in?" Without hesitation, his mother fell for the bait hook, line, and sinker and took Charles to Bed Bath & Beyond. Unfortunately, she took our checkbook with them.

They started in Aisle One with one cart and had to get a second cart by Aisle Three. In total, they spent a skillion dollars. The sales receipt was more than a yard long! They bought hangers and sheets and pillows and about half of everything else in the store. And a coffeemaker, of course.

In actuality, Charles should probably have gone shopping with his brother or someone else who had a better understanding of the true needs of a single guy living alone. For example, Charles clearly did not need a mixing bowl, a measuring cup, or an eggbeater, given his less-than-advanced cooking skills. There were also other items that will not get the intended use. For example, Mrs. Foster bought him a complete set of eight place settings, as if he might have eight people over for dinner. There is very little chance that they will ever get used as a group. However, he will use one fork a day for eight days and leave them in the sink, dirty. Then, the eight spoons, and so on. She also purchased him a full set of Tupperware to save food after dinner. What she doesn't understand is that single-guy food is either: (1) entirely consumed or (2) left on the counter for several days until the ants and the moss accumulate.

In the end, Charles settled into his first apartment and seems quite happy. Since then, Mr. and Mrs. Foster have discovered that their huge investment in Bed Bath & Beyond was not necessarily a wise outlay of savings. We visited with him a while back and got this report: He doesn't use the coffeemaker, cups, or spoons because there is a Dunkin' Donuts across the street. He doesn't do any cooking because he is usually too tired after work, and there are so many good takeout places nearby. As best we can gather, his stove has never been used. This also applies to the flatware, dish towels, dishwashing fluid, and everything else related to cooking. Also not being used is the clothes-washing equipment, hangers, or iron, or anything that revolves around keeping clothes neat or clean.

With the dirty dishes, empty refrigerator, dilapidated furniture, and clothes lying on the floor, the apartment had a familiar look to it. As we departed, I turned to Mrs. Foster and said: "It looks just like my first apartment."

No Kidding

I normally don't rent out my newspaper column space, but the Aggravated Adolescents Association of America has hired me to represent their views.

This youth group has had difficulty getting access to mainline newspapers. As a result, it has been unable to communicate with the older generation, and especially to a specific group within that generation: parents. Since I have reviewed the group's complaints and judged them to be valid, I am printing them below:

THE AGGRAVATED ADOLESCENTS ASSOCIATION'S LIST OF THE TEN MOST COMMON CRIMES AGAINST KIDS

1. *Telling Us to Do Something Without Telling Us Why*: When you are trying to get us to do something, too frequently parent types fall back on the old expression: "Because I said so." If there is a reason we should do it, tell us. If not, get off our case. If your boss at work told you to do something but refused to tell you why, you'd be mad.

2. *Trying to Make Us Dress Like You—We're 16, You're 42:* I know you want us to go to school in clean, button-down, long-sleeved shirts and pleated skirts, but that's not what kids are wearing today. We understand the torn jeans and T-shirts look slovenly to you, but to our friends, that's cool.

3. *Using Trite Expressions With No Meaning:* Don't tell us: "This is going to hurt me more than it's going to hurt you." Or "Do you think I enjoy yelling at you?" Or "I'm doing this for your own good." I know your parents used these hackneyed phrases, but they don't mean much, and we're sick of them!

4. *Setting a Bad Example for Us, or Don't Do Things You Tell Us Not to Do*: Why is it acceptable for you to have a few beers after work and then drive

home? If we did that, you would have a fit, ground us for eight years, and not let us talk on the phone for a century.

5. *Don't Cop Out: Don't ever say:* "Go ask your mother." Or "I'd let you go to the party, but your father feels strongly." It would be better for everyone if you just said, "No," and left it at that.

6. *Don't Compare Me With the Neighbor's Kids*: I'm me. They're them. If you like them better, ask the neighbors if you can adopt their kids.

7. *Don't Embarrass Me in Front of My Friends*: I'll give you a kiss and a hug in the privacy of the house but not in front of the entire school. Don't call me by your pet nickname in front of all my friends. If you call me "Cuddles," they will kid me forever.

8. *Don't Put Me Down to My Face and Praise Me Behind My Back*: Don't make threats like "You'll never get into any college" or "You'll never amount to anything in life" and then tell all your friends how great I am.

9. *Let Me Act My Age*: I know you wish I'd act more mature, but don't rush me. I'm a kid, not an adult. Would you prefer that I act forty now and like a thirteen-year-old when I am forty? I don't think so.

10. *Don't Act Surprised When We Act Like Kids*: Do you not remember anything from when you were our age? I'm sure you tried smoking and other things, too. Did you have long hair and a hippie look? I bet you weren't like Bill Clinton—I bet you inhaled. If you did these things when you were a kid, why are you so surprised when we do the same type things? It's what kids are supposed to do. You shouldn't be surprised—and you shouldn't overreact.

The Aggravated Adolescents Association's final message to parents: Yes, Mom and Dad, this is a difficult time, but I am sure we will get through it. If you could just look at things from our perspective from time to time, we wouldn't need to take over Herb Foster's column in the newspaper to communicate with you.

No Daughters for Him

Thank God I never had daughters. I know my detractors will think that this is another sexist, antifemale comment by Foster, but it's not. Actually, it's a statement about myself. In truth, I am admitting to weakness.

You see, my lovely wife and I have two wonderful boys, and I never found raising them to be overwhelming. Challenging at times, but not overwhelming. I enjoyed them when they were growing up, and still enjoy them, although they are out of the house and doing their own things these days.

However, when I speculate on what it would have been like if I had daughters, I shake at the prospect. I realize that I have some redneck blood in me, and being the father of a female would boil this blood to the surface. I realize that while I consider myself to be modern and liberal-minded, I would be old-fashioned, conservative, and obstructive if I had daughters.

To start with, I'm afraid I'd be a little restrictive regarding clothes. I understand that skintight outfits are the rage, that bare midriffs are cool, and shoes with eight-inch-high platforms are hip, but not for a Foster girl. If I had a daughter, I would allow her to wear these outfits in her room only. Whenever she left the house, she would be wearing loose-fitting clothes that cover as much skin as possible, and sensible shoes (like sneakers).

The same would apply to makeup. I understand that when a girl gets to be twelve or thirteen, she wants to put on lipstick, eyeliner, and junk like that, but I don't think it would be really appropriate for my daughter until she was at least eighteen. Maybe at age sixteen she could wear a little lipstick for special events, but not every day. The same age restrictions would apply to pierced ears—and forget about piercing any other body part!

The thought that really scares me is how I would act when my daughter started dating. My initial reaction is that a daughter of mine could not date until she was twenty-one, and even then she'd have to be home at 9 p.m. I can't imagine how I would handle having a sixteen- or seventeen-year-old boy coming to pick up my sixteen-year-old daughter to take her on a date, but I'm sure I would handle it poorly. I remember what I was like when I was sixteen or seventeen and what was topmost in my mind, and I don't want my daughter going out with a guy like that!

As I think about it, I realize that I would establish dating rules for my daughter that would probably look something like this:

My daughter is not allowed to be alone with a date at any time. There must always be adult personnel around, preferably policemen, clergymen, or nuns.

I will sew my daughter's clothes together before she leaves the house, and I will closely inspect each thread when she returns to ensure no alternations have been made.

Before daughter and date head out the front door, I expect a minute-by-minute itinerary, including addresses and descriptions of all establishments to be visited, and names and phone numbers of chaperones.

My daughter is not allowed to ride in the car of anyone who has not had a license for at least five years, nor anyone with a blemished driving record. Cars that can't go over forty miles per hour are preferred.

My daughter is not allowed to go to anyplace where there might be disreputable people present, such as music concerts, private parties, or any kind of social gathering.

Movies are acceptable, as long as the movie is PG-rated, has no romantic scenes, or anything remotely suggestive (by *my* definition).

My daughter is not allowed to talk to anyone who would even consider drinking a beer or smoking a cigarette. Random tests will be conducted.

If you do not have my daughter home within thirty seconds of her curfew, I will call the police and report my daughter kidnapped.

You can understand why I am happy I never had daughters. Clearly, I would not have been a good father, and I'm sure that all the daughters reading this are happy, too. Happy that I wasn't their father!!

A Graduated Miracle

It's a miracle. A pure miracle. I want to sing the Hallelujah chorus! I feel like dancing in the streets and kissing strangers. Why do I have this great joy?

My son, Charles, has graduated from college.

Now, before I get to describing why this was a miracle, I need to tell you something about Charles. Clearly, college should not have been challenging for him. He is plenty smart and has a good head on his shoulders. He is also one of the most wonderful, caring individuals on the planet. Everyone who meets him likes him, and he doesn't have a mean bone in his body. In general, he's a great kid.

However, his priorities in college were not necessarily education-oriented. Priority #1 was beer. Beer was the foundation on which all college was based. Priority #2 was fun. Priority #3 was his fraternity, which featured a great deal of priorities 1 and 2. Priority #4 was girls, clearly a good accompaniment to all previous priorities. Priority #5 was fraternity parties and all parties, in general. Priority #6 was friends, fraternity pals, sorority ladies. Priority #7 was fast food, such as pizzas or burgers, washed down with large quantities of #1. Priority #8 was TV, video games, and beer-drinking games.

I won't go on. I think you get the idea. We'll be into triple-digit priorities before we get to anything related to education, learning, courses, or books. As a matter of fact, some of those nasty things, like exams and papers, got in the way of his true priorities.

Another obstacle for Charles not having a cum laude college career was the school's unfortunate habit of scheduling classes during the day, especially the morning. Charles's peak performance hours are between 10 p.m. and 3 a.m., but the deans stubbornly refused to schedule classes during those hours.

This was compounded by the fact that science and industry have yet to invent an alarm clock with sufficient power to awaken young

Charles in the morning. We have tried vibrating clocks, plastic monkeys beating drums, and rock music loud enough to be heard in surrounding states. But these have no effect on the sleeping lad. Needless to say, any courses scheduled before noon were a hit-or-miss proposition for him, with a higher percentage in the miss category.

Another issue that reared its ugly head on the way to a diploma was money. Once Charles turned twenty-one and got a serious girlfriend, he started paying for dates, dinners, beverages (see priority #1), and the allowance he got from his cheap parents didn't cover his expenses. He started delivering pizza to earn spending money, but this interfered with priorities 1 through 8. It also occurred during, and took higher priority over, whatever little homework or study time that might have been allocated.

He also became president of his fraternity, and then president of the all-important Inner-Greek Council. Now, I understand that priority #3 was fraternity, but these important positions consumed a fair amount of time. Whenever we would call and ask how college was going, he would tell us about pledging events, rush parties, or fraternity field trips—never a mention of courses, grades, or anything silly like that.

We thought for a long time that Charles was on the five-year plan. He would start a semester with five courses, and then, about halfway through, he would discover that Course X was extremely difficult and was getting in the way of his priorities. He'd call his parents with a sob story, his gullible parents would bite, and—bingo!—the course would be dropped. Needless to say, this left him considerably short of required credits when it came close to graduation.

Statistics was one of these courses. He dropped it in the second semester sophomore year, first and second semesters junior year, and first semester senior year. Unfortunately, the statistics course was required for graduation, and young Charles ultimately ran out of semesters. He had to pass this course in the second semester of his senior year or not graduate. In addition, he had to make up all the credits for several dozen other courses he had dropped during the previous years. On top of all of the above, since he was a senior, he had to celebrate his potential graduation—a fairly liquid celebration (see priority #1) that started shortly after the students returned in the fall and seemed to continue right up through graduation day.

In the end, Charles seems to have pulled it off. I'm not sure how. Last Saturday, I saw him walk up on stage in a cap and gown to shake the hand of the college president. I even have pictures to prove it. I don't know how he accumulated all the credits he needed, or how he passed all those courses without ever attending them (including statistics), or how he actually graduated without having to change his important priorities one little bit. But he did it. I think it's amazing.

No, it is more than amazing. It is a miracle.

And Now, an Important Message from Your Sponsors

The following is an open letter to our two grown children who are in their midtwenties, have jobs, and live in Boston. Actually, this is in response to some specific questions regarding the house they used to call "home" and their current standing in relation to that abode.

• Yes, your room is still your room. We have kept your posters on the walls and your beer mugs on the bookshelves. However:

• One of the rooms has had a desk added to it and is now your mother's home office. She will move the papers off the second bed in the room when you come to visit, but she will ask politely that you do not disturb all the neat piles on the desk itself. She will still want to sneak in and check her e-mail when you are here, but she will refrain from doing so before 9 a.m. (One word of advice: DO NOT put beer cans on her desk!)

• The other room is, unfortunately, near the stairs to the attic. Originally, it was a staging area where items were placed prior to being moved to their final resting place. Now it has become an extension of the attic, with boxes piled up in the corners near the stairs. We are pretty sure you can get into your bed, but we ask that you be careful so you don't knock over one of the stacks of cartons.

• Yes, we love to have you visit. However, you must realize that we have been empty nesters for some time now, and we're not quite as flexible (read: tolerant) during your visits as we should be. We have a few "guidelines" you should be aware of prior to your stay:

• We play music only occasionally, and then at a very low volume. You should try to follow our good example while visiting.

• Ditto for the TV. We see no need to have MTV or the sports channel running continuously.

• You will be surprised by this news, but we actually have garbage bins in the kitchen where empty cans and trash should be disposed.

• Yes, you can bring your dirty laundry. Your mother is a sucker and will wash it for you. However, your father thinks you are taking advantage of this situation if taking the dirty clothes out of your car requires more than two trips or can only be lifted by two people. (Note regarding laundry: Your mother will wash only those clothes left in the vicinity of the washing machine. She will not pick up smelly socks from the bathroom floor.)

• Accompanying houseguests need to be approved in advance, both in terms of numbers and general character. Invitations should be issued only after detailed resumes have been provided and background checks completed.

• Visits to your wonderful parents should be kept manageable in duration. Two days is a good general guideline. A third day is OK, as long as you are mindful of the general standards published in this letter.

• However, we insist that you visit during all holidays—Christmas, Thanksgiving, etc.—and any parent birthday ending in a 0 or 5. We understand that your spouse has family, too, and might request time over the same holidays, but we are sure you can resolve this issue to our satisfaction. We realize that you might have to spend Christmas Eve with one family and then drive for hours to the second family, but we did it once and now it's your turn. (Note: Above visit-duration guidelines do not apply during holidays.)

• If you are single and bringing a person of the opposite sex, we will give each of you your own room. I know you share an apartment in Boston, but you have to understand that your parents are old-fashioned. This is the way we do things. Smile and accept it (or sneak in after we have gone to bed). When you get married, you can share a room.

• We are happy you have moved into a new apartment in Boston that's larger than your previous pad. However, we are not running the Foster Furniture Store. Any furniture that you find in the basement, attic, or garage is yours. We will help you carry it to the car. Any furniture that currently resides in any main room of the house belongs to your parents, and no amount of begging or pleading will allow it to change ownership.

• We are also more than pleased to give you a little spending money as you leave for Boston (provided you do leave). We are also happy to take you and your friends out to dinner. However, you are no longer sixteen. We will not give you our credit cards for a day of clothes shopping or a run to the music store to buy a hundred new CDs.

• Finally, and most importantly, given the acceptable-visit duration described earlier in this document, moving in is not something you should contemplate. If you find a new job in our area, you can stay with us while you seek suitable accommodation. However, in the second month, we will begin charging rent and requesting contributions for groceries, and of course, you will have to do your own laundry.

• These guidelines and visitation standards remain in effect until we get old and doddering, at which point we will happily move into your house. We would then expect to be able to play our music loudly all day, have as many visitors as we want, ask you to give us money, and do our laundry. Obviously, none of the rules covered in this letter will apply when we move into your house.

I'm a Mess

Open Mouth, Insert Foot

If there's anything I'm good at, it's putting my foot in my mouth. Truly.

If there is a room full of people and only one person in the room is going to say the wrong thing, it will be me. If a party is going perfectly and then one bad comment ruins the mood, I'll have said it.

I'm the guy who asks a woman: "How's your husband?" and she replies: "I have no idea. We're divorced."

I'm the dolt who tells someone that they have a spot of dirt on their face, and the person replies, "It's a birthmark."

I'm the fool who asks the woman with the protruding belly: "When are you due?" The woman replies: "I'm not pregnant."

Trust me. I am really good at this.

When someone gives me a present, I say: "I hope this is not a tie. I have a million ties." You know, of course, what's in the box.

When my wife gets into the car, I say: "What's that awful smell?" Her reply: "My new perfume. Glad you like it."

When I run into someone I haven't seen for a while, I say: "Have you lost weight?" The person replies: "No, I've gained twelve pounds. Thanks for reminding me."

It requires real skill to consistently offend people, but if there was an Olympics for Foot-in-Mouth, I'd be a gold-medal winner.

For example, I will be talking to a guy, and I'll say: "I can't stand men who wear those snooty Gucci loafers." The man I am talking to looks down at his feet. Want to guess what he is wearing?

You won't believe how difficult it is to walk with both feet in my mouth, but I have to do it all the time.

I'll be standing at the entrance to a party, and I'll say to a stranger: "Some idiot left his lights on." The man asks what kind of car. I tell him, and he says: "It's my car."

I want to crawl in a hole when I say these things, but usually there is no hole available, so I continue to babble and in the process put my foot in my mouth several more times. It is ugly.

Not only do I say the wrong things, I say them at the wrong time as well. There can be a large group in a room, and for some reason a silence descends just as I make some pathetically stupid comment. Everyone stares at me.

Or I'll say: "Did you see the outlandish outfit that June is wearing?" and everyone I am talking to starts making movements with their heads and pointing. I turn around, and whom do I see standing right behind me? June!

My tendency toward foot-in-mouth disease has made me somewhat reluctant to open my mouth at all, but this gets me in trouble, too. I think a coworker has a new hairstyle, but I'm too afraid to say anything. After a while, the coworker finally storms over to my desk: "Thanks for the compliments on my new hair color. You could have at least said something, dummy!" You see, I can't win.

If you have any doubts about my world-class ability, let me tell you about the Herb "Foot-in-Mouth" Hall of Fame incident. I'm standing at an office Christmas party with a man I really don't know well when suddenly a woman comes out of the crowd in our direction. I say to the man, "Whoa, look at that woman. Boy, is she built! Do you think she might come over here and talk to us?" Actually, the woman walks right up to us, and the man says, "Herb, have you met my wife?"

Foot-in-mouth disease is a terrible affliction. Try your best to be kind when you encounter a victim—like me. We know not what we say.

Sniff, Sniff, Blow and Blow

If you see a strange-looking creature walking down the street, with big red eyes and a massive runny nose and making loud woofing noises, don't be alarmed. It's just little old me with my allergies.

Every year in the springtime, when the grass turns green and the flowers come to life, I become a coughing, wheezing monster. When all the trees burst forth and the air gets thick with pollen, I become miserable. Spring and early summer is a wonderful time of year for everyone except those of us with allergies.

For several months, I am not so fun to have around (that's assuming I'm fun to have around at other times). I sneeze a lot, frequently with numerous sneezes in succession. My nose runs continuously, so I am always sniffing and looking for tissues. My eyes get red and swollen. It looks as if I have been in a prizefight. (I tell people that my wife beats me; at least I get some laughs out of my misery.)

My doctor, who I think is an excellent physician, does not seem to have a cure for me. Over the years, we have tried numerous medications, some with no effect and some with partial effect. We have finally settled on two pills a day—one in the morning, along with a nasal spray, and one in the evening. This combination keeps me somewhat livable. If I spend the afternoons inside, I sneeze only occasionally (every minute or so). My eyes get red and swollen, but I can still see out of them. (I use eyedrops, but don't tell my doctor.)

I have spent considerable time with knowledgeable authorities and sources—all the fellow allergy sufferers I meet on my travels. (Since we all have red eyes and dripping noses, we are easy to spot.) I have experimented with numerous pills, herbs, exercises, and other home remedies—all strongly recommended for "instant relief"—and all with little or no effect.

This year, I decided to do some research on allergies and tapped into the ultimate information source: the Internet. I found several sites packed full of information. I learned that my running nose is actually allergic rhinitis and my itchy eyes are really allergic conjunctivitis. It was very interesting, indeed, but not at all helpful in solving the problem. It's good that I have names for these things, but the symptoms are still there.

Finally, I found the Web site with complete instructions on how to reduce my allergic reactions. Here is the advice it provided:

• Stay indoors in the morning. (That's an excellent idea. My boss loves it when I get to work at noon every day.)

• Avoid chores that worsen your symptoms. (Yes, of course. And who, may I ask, is going to mow the lawn? The dog?)

• Do a thorough housecleaning. (Good idea. When I clean the house, I stir up everything, and my allergies get worse.)

• Monitor air-quality reports on the radio and TV. (And if I hear the air quality is bad, am I supposed to hide under my bed or something?)

• Listen for pollen-count reports. (Why do I need formal pollen count? I can tell how bad things are by the redness in my eyes.)

• Do not touch your eyes. (My eyes are stinging and itching like crazy, and you think I can keep my hands away from them?)

• Give a wide berth to certain plant life, such as oak, western red cedar, elm, birch, ash, hickory, poplar, sycamore, maple, and walnut. (I live in Bedford Hills, New York. I am surrounded by these trees everywhere I go. How am I supposed to give these things a wide berth?)

• Avoid the worst allergy culprits: pollinating grasses and trees. (This stuff is in the air, floating by, and covering my outdoor furniture. What am I supposed to do? Not breathe?)

• Steer clear of weeds such as ragweed, sagebrush, and pigweed. (I don't play in the weeds a lot anyway, but I also have no idea what a pigweed looks like.)

As you can tell, the ultimate source, the Internet, was no help at all. In the end, I have come to the conclusion that there is nothing I can do. We can land a man on the moon. We can make a computer so fancy that I can't figure out how to operate it. But we can't help people like me with allergies. I guess I'll just have to suffer and walk down the street blowing, wheezing, sneezing, dripping, and all the rest!

No Speaka le Language

Some people are good at languages, and some are not. I am definitely in the "not" group. I have zero aptitude for foreign languages. I can't speak them. I can't understand them. I am speechless in all languages but English (and people tell me my English is somewhat questionable as well).

I took two or three years of French in high school (about a hundred years ago), and I now remember two words: *oui and merci.* That's it. For all the investment my parents made in trying to educate me, all I can say is "Yes, thank you." Oh, I partially remember a bunch of words, but I have discovered over the years that a partial memory is very dangerous. In one of the few remaining brain cells in the back of my mind, I vaguely recall that bathroom in French is *salle de bain*, but if I have to go wee-wee in France and ask for that, they will show me to a room with a bathtub in it but no toilet. Embarrassing, to say the least!

Even when I remember something, my feeble attempts at pronunciation make the natives laugh and my wife wince. If I try to say *beaucoup,* what comes out of my mouth is "bow cups" or "boo coops." When a person does something for me, and I say "*Merci beaucoup,*" he almost always breaks out laughing.

When I try to order in a French restaurant, my wife tries to hide under the table. I can't even pronounce the shortest, simplest words: *eau* (water), *oeuf* (egg), *beurre* (butter), or *pain* (bread). As you can see, either the waiter speaks English or I don't get breakfast. Actually, when I am in a foreign country, my wife prefers that I not speak at all. She, of course, is a natural with languages and can communicate easily wherever she goes. And to further embarrass me, one of my sons speaks Russian and French, and the other speaks Spanish. When I am with them and try to open my mouth, they muzzle me quickly.

When I am in a foreign country, I shrug a lot. As an example, let's say a native speaks to me in rapid-fire fashion, and I don't understand a word.

If I say, "I don't speak the language" in English, he won't understand; and if I try to say the same thing in his language, he still won't understand. I can't say *oui* because he might be asking me if I want a sardine and anchovy sandwich. So I put this dumb expression on my face and shrug.

Actually, I have mastered this silent, dumb routine pretty well. If I want something, I point at it. I look at a menu for words I recognize, like *omelet,* and make no attempt at trying to pronounce it, as even a simple word like that is sure to draw smirks. This works, and I am not embarrassed. My wife tells me I am really good at this dumb routine.

I also nod a lot. If I vaguely understand the situation or question and think an affirmative answer is correct, I smile and nod. For example, a waiter approaches the table and rattles off about a thousand words in ten seconds. If I think he is asking if my meal is acceptable, I smile and nod. Unfortunately, sometimes the waiter is asking me if I want a plate of goat-intestine sausages.

So you can imagine what it is like for me in a foreign country. I spend my time looking dumb, shrugging, nodding, and pointing at things. I am not allowed to speak in public, so my wife speaks for me, orders off menus for me, and leads me around, telling me what to do. Actually, now that I think about it, I realize this is not so different from my life in the U.S. At least here I can speak some of the language.

One Rat, Pack Style

I have admitted previously to many character flaws, but now I have to add one more to the list: I'm a pack rat. Not only am I a pack rat, but I'm the worst kind: a sentimental pack rat.

My office looks like a cluttered flea market. There are mementos covering every available surface, knickknacks on the windowsills, and other paraphernalia hanging on the walls. I realize it looks a little junky, but I just can't bear to part with any of these valuable objects.

Piled on top of the TV are about thirty baseball hats. I wear the same hat almost exclusively (Bill Fisher Tackle, faded and comfortable), but the rest are far too important to be put in the trash. One from a great trip to Montana, one from the Otter Creek Brewery (reminds me of great times in Vermont), and another…I guess I don't need to go on. You can see why they are so valuable.

Hanging on the wall is a dollar I won from my nephew on the golf course, meaningful because of extensive prematch taunting; one half of a necktie, cut off in a saloon in Texas that forbids tie-wearing; a pair of Red Sox pajama bottoms that I (an avid Yankee fan) was forced to wear after losing a bet. These items have way too much sentimental value to be discarded.

I have a boomerang perched on a windowsill (trip to Australia), a noose hanging off the corner of a picture (given to me by employees), and above the desk, an old Christmas card of our Labrador Murphy (the world's best dog) that we sent out several years ago. I can't give any rational reason why I retain and display these things, except that I simply like keeping them. I think they add a little color and fun to my office. My bride thinks I work in a junkyard.

Needless to say, my file drawers are not much better, and include a two-inch-thick file on our trip to Europe three years ago, complete with maps that are surely out of date; all the tests from a first-responder course I took in 1996; and the instruction manuals from dozens of appliances (some of which have long been replaced). I keep many things because I am convinced they are going to be useful to somebody, someday.

In the closet is a large box, stuffed full of old technology stuff: cables, cords, chargers, and a bunch of things that I have no idea what they are. I am convinced that I will need something in that box very soon or that one of the chargers will replace a lost item. I realize that no two appliances use the same charger and that most of the stuff in there is antiquated, but still I keep them just the same.

You see, one of the difficulties of being a pack rat is that cleaning (read: discarding) is very challenging. For example, my "pen drawer" was getting more and more cluttered every day, to the point that it has become difficult to close. However, when I pulled it out to start organizing (read: discarding), the first three things I came across were a very handy laser-pointer thingy I used to use regularly, an Olympic pin from Lake Placid from when we saw the torch run, and a golf ball signed by Fred Couples. Now, I ask you, how could someone possibly throw any of those valuables away?

The worst, of course, is my bedside table. As I was writing this piece, I decided to take a moment to look through the drawer. I was amazed by all the wonderful things I found: a fly reel, old golf balls (too beaten up to be played with again, but from a course in Scotland), converters for European electricity, an alarm clock that needs batteries, a message in a bottle from St. John, ivory dice (lucky ones, I'm sure), and much more. It was exciting to sift through all those great collectibles.

I'm certain that some people are reading this and thinking: "This man has serious mental problems." While I have never argued with that statement, I also think it shows a lack of understanding of how a pack rat's mind works. If a pack rat comes across a single cuff link, he keeps it on the theory that the other cuff link might be found someday, or the cuff link might prove useful in some other way—someday. If, when wrapping a present, a four-inch square of paper is left over, a normal person discards it. A pack rat keeps it because it might come in handy. An old pocket watch once owned by Grandfather is way too sentimental to be discarded, and it will be taken to the shop to be repaired—someday. A pack rat has a good reason for keeping everything.

Books cause terrible problems. I can't stand to throw away books, so my bookshelves get filled to capacity, with volumes and volumes heaped on top, on the sides, and the floor. I also have large stacks of magazines and articles I want to read. I know I will never read them all, but they are too full of interesting things to be thrown away.

The only advantage of being a pack rat is that occasionally people will stop by to see if I still have something, knowing that I keep absolutely everything. "Do you still have pictures from Cindy's birthday trip to Bermuda in 1992?" Do I have them? I'm sure I do! The chances are very high that I kept those documents. Unfortunately, one of the downsides of being a pack rat is that I have a lot of stuff. A lot. And since I am not the most organized pack rat, I frequently have trouble finding specific items.

So don't count too heavily on me finding a picture from Cindy's birthday trip to Bermuda in 1992. Just know that Herbert, the pack rat, has it somewhere and that he will come across it—someday. When he does, he might consider discarding it, but after a moment's thought, he'll keep it, probably for sentimental reasons.

I'll Do It Next Week, for Sure

One thing I'm really good at is postponing. I can put off almost anything with ease. What's more, I do it in a way that allows me to nap on Saturday afternoons with a clear conscience, as if all projects were completed.

I classify my jobs around the house into several categories—This Afternoon's, Tomorrow's, Next Week's, and Next Year's. I move projects back and forth between these groups as needed.

I do not have a classification for work to be done Now. For example, I get up on a Saturday morning, and my beautiful wife announces, "I can't get my car into the garage. When are you going to clean the garage?" If I say "Today," she waits for me to start the job. However, if I say, "Tomorrow," then I have a full twenty-four hours for something else to come up that will force me to postpone the work.

As you can imagine, straightening up the garage is a job I've postponed about two hundred times. Cleaning the attic has been postponed about a thousand times. I tell you, this is something I'm really good at.

Actually, what's important is not the number of times a job is postponed but how it is put off. As with any acquired skill, technique is important. Just saying "I don't feel like cleaning the garage today" is simply not adequate.

One good technique for avoiding work is the distraction method. Say you pull up the garage door to take out the wheelbarrow and notice that the tire is flat. You spend thirty minutes taking off the tire, an hour downtown getting it repaired, an hour at the coffee shop visiting with friends, one hour resting from all the hard work, and—presto!—there's no time left to clean the garage.

Or you sneak your way through all the mess to find the golf clubs in the back of the garage. You spend three hours cleaning the clubs and organizing the golf balls and shoes. It's a job that really needs to be done.

If your wife is watching, explain the job you are about to undertake will force you to give up something she—or the kids—wants to do. It's hard for her to insist that the garage be cleaned when the kids are begging Daddy to take them to the carnival.

Another way to postpone things is to reach the end goal without doing the job itself. If your wife complains about not getting her car in the garage, go in with a shovel and move everything aside, so there's just enough room for the car. The garage has not been cleaned, but she can get her car in—what can she say?

This technique works well with the attic. When the boss asks me to take something up there, I put it at the top of the attic steps. When this area is full, subsequent items are put on the stairs themselves. When it gets impossible to get near the stairs, she insists I clean the attic. I'll go up there and move everything further back so there is room at the top of the stairs. Then I start the process all over. The goal is achieved, but the job has been postponed.

Sometimes if you put off the work long enough, you avoid the job altogether. My wife will say repeatedly, "The shutter is loose and rattling," and I will say, "I'll get to it next week." This routine goes on until one day, the boss will announce, "The shutter fell off, and the frame is cracked," and I'll answer, "Ok. I'll get a new one—next week."

This technique has worked well with the garage. When we first built the structure, it was a nice two-car garage with a small storage area. After a year, it had become a nice one-car garage with a large storage area. Now, I have postponed cleaning it so long that it has turned into a storage building, and we park both cars outside.

I'm fairly happy with this solution, but my wife the real-estate agent is still after me to clean the garage. To keep the peace, I tell her I'm going to do it. "Next week," I say. "Next week, for sure."

A Down-market Kinda Guy

I have decided that I am a down-market kind of guy. No way am I a Mercedes-driving, foie gras–eating, cuff links–wearing fella. Put me in the hamburger and beer category, thank you.

My favorite hors d'oeuvres are pigs in a blanket. Caviar on point toast is fine for some, but give me little doggies in dough anytime. I'll take chicken fingers or jalapeño poppers over watercress canapés any day of the week.

If I want to buy a cup of coffee, I go to the local store and buy a plain old-fashioned coffee. I am not big on those double-espresso, caramel macchiato mocha lattes that cost around $6.

My restaurant preferences run from reasonably priced Italian—not fancy—to expensive French. (The all-night diner is great, too!) I like cheeseburgers (with fries, of course) more than beef Wellington. When it comes to wine, I like a $15 bottle of Chianti. A $100 bottle of wine is wasted on me. I can't tell the difference between it and my cheap Chianti.

I am not a fancy dresser. I wear khaki pants about 90 percent of the time and blue jeans about another 9 percent. The remaining 1 percent is reserved for the gray flannel pants I wear to church or when the boss lady makes me dress up. In the winter, I wear flannel shirts, and in the summer, golf shirts. I make absolutely no attempt to keep up with any fashion trends. I buy clothes because something has worn out or because I need it.

Recently, I went on a business trip to Miami, and while planning an outing to South Beach, someone suggested that I wear more stylish clothes: "Something hot; different than what you normally wear." My response: "I don't have anything like that." So, he bought me a black linen shirt with buttons down the front, which I will never, never wear again. I consider a necktie to be an implement of torture. Thank God for the casual dress code. When I go see clients, guess what I wear? Khaki pants and a button-down shirt. When it's cold, I pull on a fleece or a holey sweatshirt, not a cashmere sweater. In general, I prefer being comfortable. What's wrong with that?

Labels have never been important to me. I couldn't care less who manufactures something. I have always thought that the guys with little polo players on their shirts are only wearing them for one reason: to prove to other people that they can afford shirts with little polo players on them.

I don't drive a BMW or a Mercedes. I have an SUV so I can get around when it snows and so I can drive on the beach when I go fishing. I drive my cars until they are old and beat up. I don't care if they look shabby or if it is not the latest model. I think I am being practical. My friends think I am being provincial.

In general, my repair work around the house also tends to be down-market, and is based on the "wing it and duct-tape" school of thought. If the back screen door bangs in the wind, I fix it by putting a rubber band between the two door handles. I would rather get out my own chain saw to do tree work than hire someone to do it. (Of course, my bride has the opposite opinion. She is always happy when I return from chain-saw work with all my fingers, toes, and limbs.)

My down-to-earth tendencies apply to the gym as well. I like to play racquetball, not squash. I ride the bike as opposed to having a personal trainer. Racquetball is definitely a game that the fancy folk look down their noses at, but I don't care. What is important to me is that it is a great aerobic workout, and I like beating up on old Bruce on Tuesday mornings.

I don't like those charity balls where you pay $100 a person to get all dressed up and be uncomfortable at a table with strangers, while the organization presents a Lifetime Achievement Award to someone who then talks for thirty minutes. If you want my $100, just ask for it. I'll send you a check just to avoid the torture.

I don't understand why first class on airplanes is so special. Yes, you get more legroom, but I am a short fat guy anyway, so who cares? Yes, they bring you warm nuts in a little china container, but is that worth the extra $1,000 they charge? Not to me. I'll buy nuts at the supermarket before I leave and put them in my pants pocket to keep them warm.

Good fun for me is going to a baseball game with a bunch of buddies and sitting in the sun, drinking beer. Or cooking out around the grill on a Friday night. Or just having a beer with friends after a tennis game or a round of golf.

I love going to Ham Night at the fire department, despite the fact that I end up paying about $75 for a ham that I could get at the supermarket for $10. I enjoy volunteering with our local ambulance corps. That, to me, is providing a meaningful community service. I like knowing all the policemen and firefighters in town.

Get the general picture? I don't go to a hairdresser, I get a haircut. I like classical music, but I don't go out of my way to attend the opera. My feet are more comfortable in sneakers or Merrill's than wing-tip shoes. My reading material runs more toward *Time* magazine and *Sports Illustrated* than *GQ* or *Elite*.

And you know the best part? One of the advantages of being down-market is that it costs less. I don't have to go to Brooks Brothers to shop for fancy clothes to wear chez Antoinnette for dinner. I can sit in my comfortable chair in my jeans and sneakers, eating chicken parm and drinking my cheap Chianti. It's great being a down-market guy.

Banging Around in a Newly Blurry World

I have just entered a whole new world. It's a very fuzzy world. Many objects are blurry, and I am frequently disoriented. I would like to give you more details about this new universe, but I can't see it. I have just gotten bifocals.

By way of background: my eyesight is slightly strange overall. (Why should my eyes be any different from the rest of me?) I have one nearsighted eye and one farsighted eye. For years I survived without glasses because one eye compensated for the other. If something was really out of focus, I just closed one eye. It was easy to live with.

But as time went on and I got to be an old fogy, my eyes got worse. (Everything else was falling apart—why not my eyes?) I didn't think it was much of a problem until I noticed that whenever I read a book, I kept one eye shut the entire time. "Not good," I thought. When I couldn't read the news scroll on the TV screen, I finally decided it was time to take action.

So I went to the eye doctor, and what did he prescribe? A torture device called perpetual bifocals. I don't know what I did to make the eye doctor mad at me. I have no idea why he would want to make me suffer and stumble around like a fool, but he did.

"The way these things work is simple," he said. "You look through the top part of the glasses to see far, and you look through the bottom to see things close. From top to bottom, the range of focus changes continually."

Sounds easy, right? WRONG. I can't tell you how wrong he was.

With perpetual bifocals, you must move your head up and down to bring things into focus. So if you're trying to see something far away, you put your face down toward the ground and look through the top of the glasses. If you're trying to see something close, you put your nose up toward the ceiling and look through the bottom of the glasses.

Just this head positioning alone is awkward. Why should I have to put my face up towards the sky when I want to see something on my desk? I also look like a fool walking down the street with my head down toward my feet, peering through the top of the glasses.

In addition to the stupid head positions, I find the glasses put me in dangerous situations. Take going down steps, for example. If you put your head in a normal position to go down stairs, your feet and all the steps are a total blur. You have no idea how far away each step is from your foot. However, if you put your head down far enough to bring everything into focus, your head is buried in your chest, and you can't see anything beyond the one step you're struggling with. It's a prescription for a pile of Herb at the bottom of the stairs.

A similar danger exits outdoors. Through bifocals, a curb appears to have about the same vertical drop as the Grand Canyon. To avoid serious injury, you have to stand on the edge tentatively before negotiating the decline. In general, you move around very slowly.

Another example: Say I'm driving along and the sun gets in my eyes. I do the natural thing and raise my head. You know what that means, of course. I am now looking through the bottom of the glasses (used for close-up vision), and the whole world is fuzz. Talk about scary!

During my first week with bifocals, I got a very stiff neck (and a bunch of bruises). When I watched TV in bed, the only way I could get the set in focus was to put enough pillows behind my head so that my chin was on my chest. My head was at a ninety-degree angle to the rest of my body, and after about ten minutes the pain was excruciating. When I got to my computer, my monitor was positioned too high, so I had to bend my neck 180 degrees in the other direction (nose to sky) to read my e-mail. My neck will again never be the same.

The other problem with bifocals is that objects are only in focus if you look directly at them. If you look out the side of the glasses, everything is a blur. After a while, you learn to move your shoulders and head in one movement, and you end up looking like Lurch. This is an improvement?

After a while, I called my eye doctor and I told him I couldn't see, I was dizzy, and disoriented, I had a stiff neck, and I was constantly bumping into things. Furthermore, I was walking around like a mummy, and I was afraid to go down stairs or drive with my new glasses. You know what he said? "They take a little while to get used to." Thank you, doctor. Thank you.

So, if you see me stumbling around with my head in a weird position, banging into walls, and falling down, don't think I'm drunk. I'm just getting used to my new bifocals.

Not a Techie

I am a technology sucker, a pawn in the hands of the big high-tech companies that trick me into acquiring new products because they are the latest, and greatest. I buy them, I own them, but I don't know how to use them.

That might be a slight exaggeration, but not much. For example, I have one of those newfangled phones. When my old cell phone died, I went to the store for a replacement and ended up with one of those things–I am not even sure what you call it–that not only makes calls but keeps my calendar and address book, connects to the Internet, receives instant messages, takes pictures, sends faxes, records music, dances the jig, and a bunch of other things. What do I use it for? To make calls. There are bunches of useful applications on this gadget that I have never used because I can't figure them out. I have tried to e-mail a picture, connect to the Internet to Google something, and download a program–with no success.

Another example of my getting snookered into buying more technology than I can handle is my camera, which has multiple, multiple features. It can eliminate red-eye, shoot videos, and who knows—maybe even play "The Star-Spangled Banner." I am clueless. It has all these little symbols when you look through the viewfinder—a little sun, a flower, a lightning bolt (I believe that's auto flash, but I have never been able to make it work to find out). But as far as I'm concerned they are just decorative items. I read the manual. I went to online help. I tried, I really did, but I am clueless.

I have Tivo, too. This seemed like something an idiot like me should buy, primarily because I don't know how to set the VCR. Unfortunately, as you might expect, I can't make the Tivo work either. When I tell it to record the baseball game, I get three hours of the shopping channel. When I try to capture the presidential debate, I get two hours of a soap opera in Spanish!

Our coffeemaker is supposed to do all sorts of things: auto start, short cup, espresso, and more. But the whole thing is a mystery to me. It hurts to realize that I have a coffeemaker that is smarter than I am.

Even my watch has functions I can't operate. It is only a $39 Timex. I like it because it has a button that lights up the face so you can tell the time in the middle of the night. However, when I press the mode button, it clicks to Chrono, then one more click takes it to Timer. Now, I ask you, what is the difference between the two? I can't figure out how to make either run. If I push enough buttons in Chrono mode, it starts to run like a stopwatch, but then I can't figure out how to stop it. The watch has two other functions that I know about. One is labeled AL 1-1, but I have no clue what AL is. American League? Australian Linebacker?

Then there are my remotes. I have five. Count them: 1) TV, 2) satellite, 3) VCR, 4) DVD, 5) surround sound. Combined, they must have over a hundred buttons. I know how to operate about six of them. Someone told me I could combine them all into one universal remote, but that is way beyond my skill set—way beyond.

You see my problem? Technology companies are forcing all this stuff on me, but it's far outside my range of technical capabilities. I realize some astute readers are going to question this concept of things being forced on me. But let me ask you this: When you go to the camera store, have you ever tried to ask for a camera with no features? When you go to the cellular-phone store, do you ask for a cell phone like the ones they used to sell in 1998?

No, they don't sell old technology anymore, so I am forced to buy stuff crammed with features that confuse me and make me look stupid. I am being manipulated by the big companies, and I have no control over it. I barely get comfortable with some new thingamajiggy when a new model comes out with new features and more advanced technology that I can't understand.

My technology ineptitude is obvious to those around me when they ask me questions, such as: "Is your phone GSN?" "How many megapixels is your camera?" "Does you computer have over five hundred megabytes of RAM?" Since I have no idea, I give the same answer to all those questions is: "Well, it's the latest and greatest. It must have those things."

The sad part is I don't think I'm the Lone Ranger. I think a majority of Americans are as baffled by technology as I am. My guess is that a very small percentage of people who own my kind of camera know how to use it to capacity, and ditto for my dancing, singing phone thingy. So why do the big companies keep adding new features, new functions—things they advertise as "exciting, breakthrough technology"?

You know the answer: to make money. I know it is the American way, but if it is, how come none of the Americans can use it?

Where Was I? Why Did I Come Into This Room?

The older I get, the worse my memory gets. It has become more than just embarrassing; it has become a hindrance to my daily existence. I am constantly wandering around in a fog: looking for a list I have misplaced, forgetting something I am supposed to do, or trying to think of a word to finish a sentence.

The embarrassing part is when I experience memory issues in public situations. For example, forgetting the name of someone I know well when a group of people are waiting for me to introduce that person. Or leaving my car keys on the counter of the post office and having to walk past a long line of people to retrieve them.

It is especially embarrassing when you dial someone on the phone, and when they answer, you can't remember whom you called. Now, I've done the "walk into a room and can't remember why I went there" routine about ten thousand times, but that is just private—between me and me. But when someone answers the phone and you need to ask, "Who is this?" That's embarrassing!

I constantly lose lists, too. I leave the supermarket shopping list on the counter at home. I make an elaborate to-do list and then forget where I put it. When I leave to do errands, I make an itinerary for myself so I don't forget anything; yet when I get to the bank to "deposit check" (item #2 on my list), the check I want to deposit is sitting on my desk at home.

It has gotten so bad that I forget the most basic information. I go to the doctor's office, and they ask me who my health insurance provider is. I have no idea and have to call my wife to find out. The nurse gives me the "oh boy, what idiots I have to put up with" look.

When people ask me how long I have been married, I say, "Oh, over thirty years." I am not very clear as to the exact number. I think it is thirty-three or thirty-four years, but I could be off by a year or two either way. I also struggle to remember my kids' birthdays. One is 9/7/79; or is it 7/9/79? Or…well, you get the picture. (I forget my age, too. I know I am over forty, but beyond that, it is all a little fuzzy. I just tell people fortysomething—but I might be off by a decade or two.)

I walk into the video store and stare at the DVDs for a while, trying to determine if I have seen them or not. I can't ask the guy behind the counter if I rented them because it is possible I took them home and didn't watch them. Ditto when go to the bookstore to get books to take on vacation. I look at titles, read the descriptions and even the first few pages, but frequently, I have no idea if I've read the book or not. Recently, I bought a Dick Francis book to read on a trip. When I returned home, my young bride informed me that I had read the book before. She even showed it to me on the bookshelf! The sad part is that, even though I enjoyed the book thoroughly, I didn't remember until she reminded me.

Sunglasses are a special challenge because of all the many places they might be hiding: the car, my dresser, the tennis court, on my head. What a waste—all the hours I spend looking for my sunglasses. I always had trouble with phone numbers until I got a Palm Pilot. Now not only can't I remember the number, but I also forget where I left the Palm Pilot.

Of course, I am constantly in trouble with my wife because I only remember a fraction of what she tells me. On a Saturday morning, she will give me a long list of projects, but no sooner is her car out of sight when her list of honey-do jobs disappears into the ozone, leading up to a not-very-upbeat performance appraisal at the end of the day.

When I put something away in a "special place" to make sure I will find it later, that item is lost forever. I think, "I'll never forget that I put it here," but I won't see that item until two years later, usually, when looking for something else. I'll stumble across it and say, "Oh, that's where I put it!"

There are times when I feel just plain stupid. I get into an intellectual conversation (what the heck am I doing there?), and I can't remember who wrote *The Grapes of Wrath*. Another time, I tell a group of people that we spent two weeks in Italy, and when they ask where, my mind goes blank. There is a pregnant pause while I say: "Um...um...," but nothing is forthcoming. On my way home, it comes to me: "Lucca! Lucca!" I say out loud, but of course, it is too late. The people think I am an idiot. "He spent two weeks there, and he can't remember where?"

Then, of course, you have passwords. I have a set password I have been using for years. Unfortunately, the banks and other institutions have started implementing new rules that passwords now need to include both numbers and letters and must be changed frequently. As a result, Herb is constantly clicking the Forgot Your Password? button.

And one of the big things I forget, being a columnist for a newspaper, is column ideas. I will be somewhere and a comment will spark an idea. But unless I write it down *immediately*, it just becomes a great idea lost in the fog. I like hiding at home behind my computer where, aside from passwords, there are very few names and things to forget. I try to avoid large cocktail parties filled with people I know, 90 percent of whose names I can't remember!

I know people have many funny nicknames for my problem: "sometimer's disease," "senior moments," etc. Call it what you want, but I call it scary. However, all you readers out there can help me out. If I run into you on the street and I seem to be struggling with your name, volunteer it, please! If you see me at a social function, don't expect me to introduce you to the person next to me. If your phone rings and it's me, just tell me who you are. Don't torture me. My terrible memory is torture enough!

Food Fights

A Cold and Mysterious Place

My wife and I ventured into a foreign world last week. Together, we steeled our nerves, put on protective clothing, and entered into a dark and cold place: our freezer!

We did not embark upon this adventure lightly. We realized that it had been a long time since we'd completely emptied out the freezer (like never), and that there might be a few older items residing there. But we had something that needed to go into the freezer, and no matter how hard we tried to move things around, there simply was no place to fit it. We knew it would be a dark and dirty job. And it was.

Here is what we found:

1. A plastic storage bowl marked "spaghetti sauce." Now, not only did this container have no date on it, but neither of us could remember *ever* making spaghetti sauce. This was a sure sign that the sauce was old, very old. It went into the garbage quickly.

2. A jar with a reddish brown substance in it. It was not chili or tomato sauce or meat of any kind. What it actually was remains a mystery. We debated allowing it to defrost, but neither of us wanted to face (or smell) the item after thawing, so it, too, went into the garbage.

3. A piece of meat, also difficult to identify. It was probably lamb, but it could have been beef, venison, duck, or—who knows? It was dark, so it was probably not poultry (maybe four-year-old poultry?), but we didn't keep it around long enough for further investigation.

4. Numerous packages with poor and unclear labeling. Chicken labeled "5/4." Was that May of 2004, 2002, 1989, or before? A container with a tag that said "Lamb Stew—family ski trip—Christmas." We appreciated the excellent description, except we have been skiing during the week after Christmas for years anyears. Anything in the

vague-labeling category went into the trash.

5. Leftovers, mostly poorly marked, of all kinds. Extra spareribs. Soups, hamburger packages, chicken sausage, chili. As we pulled these items from the freezer, we kept asking, "*Why did we save this?*" Many of the items were portions too small for two people. Example: two small coq au vin chicken legs. These were not even enough to feed one person; what's more, they were obviously the pieces no one wanted when we served the dish in the first place. Good-bye.

6. Many other items went into the "what were we thinking?" category. For example: two bags of Halloween candy. Yes, we had fewer trick-or-treaters than we expected, but whose idea was it to put the extra candy in the freezer? Colored Easter eggs—was there ever really any intention that we would use these again? One small piece of ginger root, the size of one fingernail, carefully put into a freezer bag, and then wrapped in two layers of foil. By my guess, it was probably seven cents worth of ginger. As I gave it a three-point shot into the trash can, I couldn't help but think of all the electricity we had used over the years to keep that piece of ginger frozen.

7. Turkey potpies, made after Christmas a year ago. We assumed these would be OK to eat after only one year in the freezer (considering the state of the above items, "one year" deserves the modifier "only"); however, the reason we ventured into the freezer in the first place was to make room for the leftover turkey potpies from Christmas this year. Out they went.

8. All kinds of foods that we wouldn't eat anyway, even if they were fresh. Garden burgers. Low-fat burritos. Lima beans. My cute little wife and I looked at each other accusingly when we pulled each of these items from the freezer, both thinking the other person had purchased them. We blamed past diets as we tossed them out.

9. Food that represented past Foster family food fads: bean sprouts and curd from when we loved Japanese, marinated cabbage and duck sauce from our Chinese days, andouille and okra

from our New Orleans Creole phase. When I liked these foods, I was about twenty pounds lighter and my hair was not gray. These went the way of the fads.

10. A number of middle-ground items that could have been saved or could have been thrown: vegetable packages with a little bit of frost on the outside, chicken in the original supermarket package that was only four months old, hors d'oeuvres made for the cocktail party last summer. These items led to discussions about how long things last in the freezer and using up food in the freezer; from there we moved on to a longer, philosophical debate about the quality of food from the freezer versus fresh food. After this, we discarded all middle-ground items.

In the end, with the carnage completed, the freezer was empty. We had thrown everything out! The garbage was full, the freezer was bare, and we were very proud of ourselves. I was just about to put the new turkey potpies on one of the empty shelves when my wife stopped me and said: "Look at the label." It said" "Pot Pies, Christmas." Had I learned nothing from the last hour of torture? Quickly, I added the words: "Made Dec. 28, 2004." I finally felt as if I had conquered the freezer once and for all. My wife and I removed our plastic gloves and shook hands. We had conquered a dark and mysterious world.

One Man's Spin on Doing the Laundry

I hate to admit this, but there is one machine that has always baffled me: the clothes washer.

Maybe I had a poor education when I was growing up, or maybe I'm just a man, but I am at a total loss when it comes to washing and drying clothes. I can run the dishwasher (somewhat reluctantly, I admit), but when it comes to washing clothes, I am hopeless.

My wife was out of town recently, just long enough for me to develop a large pile of clothes in the laundry room. I decided I shouldn't be a total cad and leave it for her return. No, I would take a run at washing clothes.

I screwed up my courage, but as soon as I got in front of the washer, I felt as if I were looking at the control panel of a spaceship. This machine has more buttons and knobs and confusing options than a submarine dive station.

The far left dial, for example, has three different water temperatures listed: cold, warm, or hot. How do I know what's appropriate? I have a pile of clothes lying on the floor. Do I ask them: "What water temperature would you prefer?" Do I read the tag on each garment to see what it calls for? I don't think so. Warm sounded good to me.

The main dial in the center has more words around it than the average dictionary. There is a large circle on the outside with a series of wash alternatives, which are Greek to me: Regular Cycle, Permanent Press Cycle, Delicates, Pre-Wash, Extra Clean Cycle, and Auto Extra Rinse.

As a starter, I decided I could eliminate the Permanent Press option. I am not sure what "permanent press" really means, but I know I do not have any clothes that fit into the neat or "pressed" category. Now, if there was a spot on the dial for Permanently Wrinkled, I would select it immediately.

Ditto for Delicate. Since most of my apparel is large enough to fit a full-grown elephant and runs heavy in denim, "delicate" is not aword that most people would use to describe my clothes.

This left me four choices: Regular, Extra Clean, Pre-Wash, and Auto Extra Rinse. My gut feel is to go with the Extra Clean, especially since my clothes were extra dirty, but then do I need extra detergent or water? I decided it was safer to go with Regular.

Unfortunately, that was not the end of my decision-making. There was another dial that asked about water level: Low, Medium, or High? How was I to know what water level to select? Did this mean load size? I selected Medium. It seemed like the least dangerous choice.

With most of my decisions completed, I reached up to the detergent shelf, and panic set in. There was a big bottle of Tide with Bleach Alternative ("Deep Clean") and an equally large bottle of Tide with no bleach. There was a large bottle of Clorox and a box of Clorox2 detergent. And a bottle of Arm & Hammer concentrated detergent. And a bottle of Delicare ("Cold Water Wash for All Fine Washables"). And a bottle of fabric softener. And a box of Wisk Dual Action Tablets (now we're getting into the sexy stuff). And finally, a jug of Xtra, which I had no idea if it was detergent or floor cleaner.

Then I noticed a small bottle in the corner—Snuggle (the name sounds like clothes detergent for people who take Viagra). But it was the small type on the corner that worried me: "With color protection." Suddenly, I had a new concern. Colors! Could I wash all these different colors together? I looked at the pile on the floor. There were reds, blues, whites—I had no idea!

Not only did I have to decide which detergent to use, but also how much to put in. I had this image of suds pouring out the front of the machine and flooding the laundry room. A cup? Two cups? Three cups? Again, I had no idea.

As I was standing there trying to calculate which detergent to use and recalculating the settings on the machine, I looked over at the dryer. Again, I was faced with a variety of options: one dial that said things like: Auto Dry Regular, Damp Dry, Wrinkle Release; another dial that had a bunch of temperature controls; and above the dryer, another collection of options: Bounce and other products to put in with the drying clothes.

So here I was, totally baffled by all dials and possible combinations of detergents, washer settings, dryer settings, and additives. I came to the only conclusion that a man in this situation would come to: I looked at the clothes on the floor and realized they were really not that dirty after all. I selected a pair of pants from the pile, a shirt, underthingies, and socks, and sure enough, they were definitely clean enough to wear. I put them on (reducing the dirty laundry pile in the process), and headed out the door. All that worry and decision-making was for naught. Sometime soon, I would learn how to run the washing machine.

Defeated by a Turkey

Here's the score from Thanksgiving Day: Turkey 1, Herb 0.

Every year we have a big crowd for Thanksgiving dinner. Every year I get the "honor" of carving the turkey. After all the food is laid out on the table, the turkey is brought in with great fanfare. Someone says grace, and then all heads turn toward me and my carving utensils, with great expectations. I break out into a cold sweat.

The cooked turkey lying on the platter doesn't look like a stalwart opponent, but he is. I have wrestled him before and never won. He doesn't look strong, but I know he is a slippery devil, with muscles in hidden places.

This year I started off my attack by attempting to cut off one of the drumsticks. I pulled the leg back, cut through the skin, and began searching for the joint. I sawed back and forth for several minutes. Then I gave the drumstick one big pull, and out came the bone in my hand—one bare bone with no meat on it! Several people at the table started to giggle.

Giving up briefly on the legs, I turned my attention to white meat. I eyed the plump breast with some distrust, and as an opening parry, I poked the skin with the point of the knife. A buttery, greasy mixture squirted onto my tie. Round two to the bird. More people began to giggle.

I then started to carve with earnest. I drew the knife back and forth across the skin repeatedly, but the blade, which I had sharpened earlier, made no progress through the skin. I began to stab at the crust with the point of the knife until some jokester called out, "Stop stabbing the turkey! The bird is already dead."

With the skin out of the way, I established the contortionist position required to properly carve a turkey: left hand inserting the fork into the bird near the top, requiring the left elbow to point straight up into the air, while underneath this elbow, carving is done with the right hand. It was awkward, but my first slice looked pretty good, until I took the fork out of the bird and attempted to transfer the piece to a plate. Halfway between the platter and the plate, the meat fell apart into multiple shreds all over the tablecloth. More laughter around the table.

No matter how hard I tried, I was unable to get one complete, intact slice over to a plate. Most people got chunks and strands of turkey, some of which had taken a little detour to the tablecloth on the way to the plate. Some guests were holding out their plates, trying to catch the turkey pieces as they fell.

As I carved, the amount of buttery, greasy liquid on the platter increased, and the turkey began to slide from end to end on the serving plate. If I pressed too hard with the knife or fork, the movement became violent, so I was basically chasing the turkey around the platter, taking swings at it with my knife. "Put your foot on it!" someone yelled.

You can imagine the scene: My tie, my shirtfront, and a two-foot radius around the platter were covered with a mixture of turkey pieces, stuffing, and butter/grease. The people nearest me had moved their chairs back from the table and were holding their napkins up for protection.

However, the good news is that I was making progress. The carved turkey did not look great, but I was able to maneuver little pieces of meat onto about twelve plates, and I could see the end of my carving torture in sight. Unfortunately, our friend Missy asked if she could have the oysters—"the best part" she said. (You would think she would be more understanding after watching me lose the first several rounds of the wrestling match.) Bravely, I tipped the bird precariously over on its side and started cutting out the oysters, when suddenly I lost it all. The turkey slipped off the platter completely and landed on the tablecloth with a resounding thud. The platter flipped completely over, landing upside down on top of the creamed onions. Everything within two feet (including people) was covered with a mixture of turkey, butter, and stuffing. The laughter had stopped. There was now total silence around the table.

With this catastrophe, I was defeated. I laid down my carving utensils and lifted up the bird's one remaining drumstick as a sign of victory. Game, set, and match to the turkey. Far down at the end of the table, one person broke the silence to say: "What a turkey!" I'm still not sure if he was talking about the bird on the platter or me.

Losing My Senses

I have decided that I was born with inferior sensory equipment. Compared to normal people (rarely do I get put in the normal-people category), my sense of smell and taste are clearly lacking.

This deficit was especially apparent recently when an older-than-fossils friend of mine gave us a present of a case of wine designed for tasting. Each bottle was accompanied by a profile that provided detailed information on the wine, not only the producer, vintage, region, and primary grape, but also the "tasting characteristics" that I was going to experience.

Since I have always been interested in scientific experiments, I jumped right into this project (let me emphasize that my interest was strictly technical, and had nothing to do with the fact that this particular experiment involved drinking wine). The initial bottle was Cabernet Sauvignon from Napa Valley, and I went through all of the formal tasting procedures correctly. I opened the bottle carefully, allowed it to breathe, and swirled it around in the glass. The first thing we were supposed to do was observe the color. My eyes seem to be working fine: indeed, it looked like a "deep ruby red."

Then came the second test, described on the sheet as "nose." This Cabernet was supposed to have the aroma of "ripe black cherry, spicy plum, vanilla bean, and toasty oak." I swirled the wine one last time, stuck my nose deep into the glass, inhaled, and savored the bouquet. What did I smell? Wine. No cherries, plums, vanilla beans, or oak trees. Just plain old wine. Was I doing something wrong?

Next was the tasting stage, and according to the sheet, I was supposed to enjoy flavors that included "blackberries, cherries, cocoa, and spice." I tasted, swished the wine around in my mouth (no spitting, sorry), but again, no blackberries, cherries, or other fruit. It just tasted like wine to me. (I was just as happy. I'm not sure I wanted cocoa and spice in my wine.)

Maybe I didn't understand this wine-tasting thing. The sheet described the wine as "rich, structured, complex, and beautifully balanced." Since I was unsure what "complex" meant, I looked it up in a wine book, and the definition was "a wine that combines all flavor and taste components in almost miraculous harmony." While that really didn't help me understand what "complex" meant, I certainly wasn't experiencing "miraculous harmony."

But being dedicated, I forged on into the second bottle. This was a 1997 Barolo, and again, I was unable to smell the "strawberry jam, smoke, and violets" in the nose stage or savor the "sweet ripe berries and chocolate" while tasting. Now, I have to tell you, it was a spectacular wine that I enjoyed thoroughly, but obviously I was missing something in the sensory department.

On and on it went, through the third bottle—I couldn't find the "lingering velvety finish"—and the fourth—no "beautifully integrated oak"—and similarly throughout the case. At the end of the experiment, I decided that either I have been gypped in the smelling and tasting department, or these wine experts just have active imaginations (a real possibility, in my mind).

This forced me to begin to think of my other sensory shortcomings, and I realized I have the same problem with food. My wife will taste something and say, "Oh, it has a hint of saffron." Well, first off, I have no idea what saffron tastes like. Second, when I tasted the food, I couldn't detect a hint of anything. Over the years, she has given up asking me to smell the sour cream to see if it's "bad." Unless it is really gone, it will smell fine to me.

Then, of course, there are my hearing problems. I can't hear anything my wife tells me (especially when it involves a honey-do project or a dinner party), and I can't hear a thing in crowded social event. I try to use the latter issue as a solid reason why I should not attend the Garden Club of America Reception and Awards Banquet. Unfortunately, my pretty young bride does not buy that rationale and forces me to attend anyway.

You see my problems in the sensory area? Initially, during the wine experiment (an ongoing project, by the way), I thought I just had poor taste buds (my friends would say I have no taste). Now I realize that the scope of the problem includes my nose, my ears, and more. I tell you, I have been issued substandard sensory equipment, and I intend to file a complaint with the man in charge.

What's Cookin'?

My wife has this cooking thing down pat. She is able to provide dinner every evening with a minimum of fuss and bother and still fit in all her real-estate appointments, ambulance-corps business, fire-department meetings, tennis matches, golf games, nails, Quicken, e-mail, and who knows what else. You might think she is a superwoman, but actually she has just developed a great system for evening-meal preparation. The key to her system is a regular rotation of clever techniques.

Here are her six most frequent methods:

Let's Cook on the Grill: Except in the heaviest of snowstorms, my wife suggests this. I'll get a call around 6 p.m. from the boss lady, and the message will be: "There are chicken breasts in the fridge for cooking on the grill. Go ahead and stick potatoes in the oven at 350, and I'll be home after I make tomorrow's appointments."

Can You Stop on the Way Home? Again, I'll get a call around 6 p.m. The message this time will be: "Don't you feel like something a little different tonight? How about Indian food? I'll call and place the order at 7 p.m., and you can stop on your way home and pick it up." I pick up Chinese food. I stop for pizza. I even stop at the pasta place and get cooked pasta to bring home.

Gourmet Food: No call this evening. I get home around 7 p.m. and to my delight find that for dinner, we have cold poached salmon, risotto with peas and peppers, asparagus with tarragon vinaigrette, and a white chocolate mousse for dessert. These items will all be laid out beautifully on the table, and I'll be thinking: "Isn't it nice that my lovely wife went to all this trouble…" when I notice the plastic containers in the garbage. Ah ha, she stopped on the way home at the gourmet shop!

The Joneses Have Invited Us: We are often invited to our Friends' houses for dinner. It's great to see them, it's a fine way to have dinner, and my wife escapes another night at the stove. When friends come over to our house, my wife suggests I cook for them on the grill, of course.

Let's Go Out: Of course, this is the most popular dinner variation. "Let's run over to the diner for pasta." "Let's grab a quick bite at Nasty's Restaurant." Or simply, "Let's go out. What do you feel like having?" The variety is nice, but after a while this gets a little hard on the family budget.

You're on Your Own: This dinner variation frequently comes in the form of a message left on my voice mail at the office. The communication goes something like this: "I have an ambulance-corps board meeting tonight. You're on your own for dinner" or "Still showing houses. Make your own dinner." Sometimes these messages have a P.S.: "Look in the freezer."

You will note that none of the six techniques above involves my wife turning on the stove. As I said, she's really got this cooking thing down pat.

Creative Writing on the Menu

Some of the best creative writing I have ever seen is done on menus.

Truly, the people who write the descriptions of meals in restaurants rank up there with some of the greatest fiction writers of all time. They can make the most ordinary dish sound spectacular and make your mouth water in anticipation—until the meal is served, of course, and then reality sets in.

These folk don't simply put the word "swordfish" on the menu. Oh, no—they call it "pungently spiced swordfish nestled in a cool chili cream sauce." Shrimp isn't just "stuffed," it is "plump with sherried crabmeat." A combination of ribs and chicken instantly becomes "A Deep South Dixieland barbecue."

Items are not cooked, they are "grilled to perfection" or "exquisitely prepared." They don't just serve cheese; they have a "lavish presentation of international and domestic cheeses." Sauce is not just added to an item, it is "smothered succulently."

These writers are great with the adjectives. One is "jumbo." Everything is "jumbo"—jumbo shrimp, jumbo cookies, jumbo drinks, etc. When they are not using jumbo, they say "generous." You always get a generous serving of mashed potatoes (like you need them) or a "generous portion of crabmeat." Other frequently used words are: "tangy," "zippy," "delicate," and of course, "savory."

One of their favorite tricks is to add the word "gourmet" to an item. Instantly it becomes a delectable, upscale dish. Chicken is chicken, but "gourmet roasted chicken" is something special. When in doubt, the menu drafters use "gourmet."

With these writers, salad greens are always "tender," lamb chops are always "extra thick," and the wine list is always "hand-picked." Several ingredients are not just mixed together, they become a "delicate blend of perfectly cooked" something or other.

One main course is "touched with sesame seeds and onion."

Touched? Another is "lightly dusted in a cornmeal crust," and a third is "garnished with salsa." Or maybe you want lamb with "the essence of rosemary?"

Menu writers frequently double as mystery writers, developing descriptions that are less than 100 percent descriptive. One menu lists: "Yukon Gold Strike potatoes" and "delightful diver scallops." Hello? Can someone explain what a diver scallop is, and how they are different from regular scallops? Another restaurant lists: "matchless chicken paillard." Now, I have no idea what paillard is, but I am not going to embarrass myself by asking the waiter.

What is "Painted Black Bean Soup" or "Chicken Trinidad" or roasted "Baron of Beef"? (I have never eaten a baron before, and don't care to, thank you!) Do you know what "fingerling potatoes" are? Are they french fries? By the way, these writers have more ways of describing mashed potatoes than Ford has cars!

Many menus have sexy-sounding items from faraway ports—"Iowa corn-fed beef" or "Florida orangewood-smoked turkey." (What is from Florida, the orangewood or the turkey?) Do I believe these foods came from those areas? No, I think they came from the writer's imagination. Several menus have "crisp Long Island farmhouse duck." Now, I have spent considerable time on Long Island, and I have seen many cars and many buildings but not many farmhouses with ducks out front.

Restaurants also like to brag about their in-house capabilities: "served with our special secret salad dressing." Or they call it "our signature dish," or the "Specialty of the House" or the "Chef's Special." One menu says: "served with *our own* coleslaw and fries." Thank goodness it's yours. I hate to have you selling something that belongs to someone else!

Needless to say, I am not on the same wavelength as the menu writers. They think their words enhance what they call "my dining experience." In truth, I didn't come to the restaurant to have an experience. I just came to eat.

The Perils of the Picnic

Summertime food and I don't get along.

It's not that I don't like summer food—I do. It's just that I find eating it to be very difficult. I love the ribs, corn on the cob, barbecued chicken, greasy cheeseburgers, the whole works, but I find it very challenging to consume these items without making a major mess—on me, my clothes, the tablecloth, and everything else within a six-foot radius.

Say you go to a dinner party, and they serve ribs. Everyone knows the only way you can successfully get the meat off the bone is to pick up each rib individually, wrestle with it, and in the process cover approximately 50 percent of your body with barbecue sauce. A napkin is clearly an insufficient cleanup tool after ribs. What you really need is a shower.

Now, consider hamburgers. I love cheeseburgers all junked up: ketchup, mustard, onion, lettuce, tomato, pickles, and relish—everything I can stuff between the buns. While the end result tastes great, it leaks all over the place. Little bits of mustard, relish, and all the rest drop onto the front of my shirt, my pants, my shoes, and the person sitting next to me.

Have you ever arrived somewhere and have the hostess say: "We have a special treat tonight. We're having lobsters." Great! Every time I crack a lobster claw, juice flies ten feet in all directions. That's why the only way I like to eat lobsters is in a bathing suit.

To make matters worse, these foods are frequently served with the favorite summer vegetable: corn on the cob. I don't know about you, but as I munch my way down the cob, only about 30 percent of the corn gets into my mouth. The rest gets stuck in my teeth! When I smile, all you see is bright yellow corn kernels.

Sometimes it is not the food itself but how it is served that gives me problems. I hate it when I'm invited to a function and they serve dinner on paper plates with plastic utensils. Try cutting up a tough steak or barbecued chicken with a plastic knife and fork. It is impossible not to create a mess. Most of these paper plates are as rigid as a sheet of toilet paper, so when you put a scoop of potato salad on one side, it rolls right off onto your shoe.

Recently, I went to a party where they served shish kebab. Now, how difficult could that be? Well, the skewer was hot, and in the process of trying to get the food to my plate, I dropped most of it in my lap. At another party, I was served a taco, and when I took my first bite, it crumbled into a million pieces, a virtual explosion of Mexican food all over me.

When you are invited for a cookout, you can't go in totally grubby clothes or take a plastic bib and a dozen toothpicks. No, as you put on a clean shirt and pants, you know they are going to the dry cleaners the next day. As you shower, you realize that your hands, arms, face, etc. will soon be covered with various food particles and barbecue sauce.

After a meal, it is very easy to tell what was served—just look at my shirtfront. When I go to the dry cleaners, Mr. C. says to me: "I see you went to another barbecue over the weekend. They must have served hot dogs. I can see the mustard stains and tomatoes. Here is a red stain and a seed."

When I go to a picnic, I am an instant magnet for yellow jackets. Everyone around me can be fine, but I will be sitting in a buzzing swarm. If I go to a beach party, I get sand in my food. No matter how careful I am, I crunch when I eat (boy is that fun).

Got the picture why I have trouble with August eats? Barbecued food trickles sauce, sandwiches ooze mayo, drink cans sweat, ice-cream cones drip, and limes spray juice. I do love summertime, when the living is easy. I just wish eating the food was easy, too.

An Inner-Body Battle Between the Forces of Good and Evil

There's a major battle going on inside this huge body of mine. I am basically a shell, and inside this shell are many opposing forces struggling for control and dominance. I can feel the battles going on, and I'm afraid the evil influences are winning.

Here are some of my inner-body competitors:

Consumption: The consumption army is large and has great power. With increasing frequency, it pushes aside all other forces and makes the body consume huge amounts of food—mostly carbohydrates, pizza, and the like.

Restraint: What would offset Consumption is the Restraint force. However, Restraint has no power or guts. When Consumption is making the body eat enough food for an elephant, Restraint does not have the mettle to execute basic moves, like pushing a plate away or leaving the table. There are also certain foods that Restraint cannot resist. For instance, when bread and butter are put on the table, Consumption reaches for it, and Restraint looks on as an ineffectual bystander.

Willpower: One reason Restraint has no guts is that potential partners such as Willpower are also weak. In my shell, Willpower is just one weak old guy with a lot of brainpower and very little muscle. Willpower is good at communicating—at telling the rest of the body what should be done—but has no grit when it comes to enforcement.

Exercise: In theory, Exercise should offset the Consumption forces. A good dose of strong Exercise can burn off many calories and negate the harmful effects of Consumption. It is a good theory, but Consumption is clearly winning this battle. Actually, what is happening is that the more the body exercises, the more energy Consumption gathers; it then uses this additional energy to force me to gorge myself even more. It is a losing battle.

Diet: Diet is an ever-present longing that becomes especially strong whenever the shell steps on the scale or looks in the mirror. Unfortunately, Diet is basically an idea, a concept, and has no armies itself. It requires the support of other soldiers such as Willpower or Restraint to assert itself. As noted before, neither Willpower or Restraint have any muscle, so Diet really falls into the category of a wish or a dream.

Sensible Lifestyle: Sensible Lifestyle resides in the brain and tries to get the body to do good things—get enough sleep, drink enough water, and eat plenty fruits and vegetables. It is a voice of reason among the battling forces, but sadly, that is all Sensible Lifestyle is: a voice. Background noise. Elevator music that is quickly forgotten in the presence of a bag of potato chips or a bowl of M&Ms.

Fun, Fun, Fun: These are bad-boy gangs that ride around causing trouble. They see Diet, Restraint, and Sensible Lifestyle as boring and dull. They make the world seem gray and flat when a diet is considered, and they play music when Consumption is looking at the dessert menu. They make everything brighter and more colorful when the evil fattening forces are in control.

Good Intentions: The Good Intentions (GI) army is like an inner body mom. It is always in the background saying things like, "Here is what you should do," or "Don't eat that!" Unfortunately, whenever GI is confronted by a strong opposing force, such as a butterscotch sundae, it just starts to scold and nag, which causes the evil forces to rebel and eat even more. Into the GI category go things like New Year's resolutions and similar promises made at weak moments.

Alcohol: Alcohol is a major ally of Consumption, Fun, and the other bad guys. Sometimes, the body will go into a meal with strong resolve to support the armies of Good Intentions, Sensible Lifestyle, and Diet, but after Alcohol gets involved, the voices of Good Intentions and Restraint disappear entirely.

Guilt: Guilt is another force out there that comes and goes like the tide. The day after Consumption has a big victory, Guilt strikes back, causing the body to feel regret, shame, and embarrassment. It partners with Good Intentions, Willpower, and Diet to issue edicts like: "Never again." Or "Today, I am going to turn over a new leaf." Unfortunately,

Guilt does not have staying power, sometimes not even lasting to the next meal, when the sirens of Consumption play again.

Sweet Tooth: Sweet Tooth (ST) is an innocent-looking little thing, very quiet and unassuming until the dessert menu is presented. Then, all of a sudden, Sweet Tooth becomes the most powerful force in the body. Show ST a menu with peppermint-stick ice cream on it, and everybody else better stand back, because ST is going to force the mouth to say: "I'll have a double portion."

I don't see an end to these battles. All the positive forces look good and say the right things, but in the end, they're no match for their more powerful opponents. All the evil forces are stronger, talk louder, have larger armies, and in general are in control. They push the body toward fattening desserts and away from the gym. They force the body to eat baked potatoes with extra butter and sour cream and seduce you away from diets of any kind. The bad forces make the body much bigger than it needs to be, and the good forces cannot do anything about it. And I am just a shell—a large shell at that.

Fighting the Good Fight

The Husband Test

Ever since I warned potential brides about husband communication issues, I have been besieged by calls and letters from young ladies asking me to pass on more advice—especially tips on what qualities to look for in a potential mate. Being a dedicated public servant, I am happy to comply.

You see, a big mistake some women make is selecting a partner without looking beyond the excitement of romance and courting. I know the love thing and wrestling stuff is very, very important, but let's get practical, ladies. You're going to spend the rest of your life with this guy. After a while, if you're lucky, the romance part turns into an ongoing warm glow. Granted, it tends to glow more on vacation in the islands and less when discussing family finances, as other aspects become more important.

So, brides-to-be, my suggestion is this: step off that love ladder for a few minutes and examine that guy like you would a dress or a pair of shoes in a store. Pretend he is on sale and give him a good, thorough assessment. Look under the hood and kick the tires, so to speak. To help you, here are a few sample questions you should ask before uttering the magic words "I do."

Is he handy? Will he be able to fix something when it is broken? Does he know which end of the hammer to hold? Is he good with power tools? Is a leaky faucet an easy fix or a $200 plumber bill?

Is he willing to cook *in the kitchen?* (Every guy is willing to cook on the outdoor grill.) Equally important to cooking is washing the dishes. Translation: Is he willing to help out in some way, or does he see the kitchen as foreign territory?

Does he know how—or is he willing—to move clothes from the washer into the dryer and push the On button? It is probably best that you not expect him to operate the washer, too. Trust me on this and don't put your wardrobe at risk.

Does he have a good job? Does he bring in half-decent bucks? The money thing is important, but some of these guys who make big buckos are never home. They leave at 6 a.m. and get home at midnight. You'll be able to buy anything you want, but do you want a credit card as your primary day-to-day companion?

Can he cope? Imagine you are driving to the in-laws with three kids in the car, ages four, two, and six months, all crying and complaining constantly. It's pouring rain, you get a flat tire, and all the luggage is piled on top of the spare. How would the love of your life handle that situation?

Does he have bad habits? Is he a golfer? Will he be gone for long periods of time on a Saturday or Sunday morning? Is he a poker player?

Does this man have any degree of soft-and-fuzziness? Is there any chance that you will get flowers from him in your fifth year of marriage?

Spend enough time together to find out if he snores, leaves toothpaste all over the sink, or drops his smelly socks on the floor. Please note, in this regard, I must advise brides not to be too picky. Men are men. You just have to decide what degree of male sloppiness you are willing to put up with.

This should give you a good idea of the questions to ask. And, by the way, don't go into a marriage thinking you can change him. The bad news is that he's been on his best behavior; he will only go downhill from here. If he leaves his dirty underwear on the floor now, he will always leave his dirty underwear on the floor.

I know it is hard to consider all these practical things right now. Today you are dating, and you spend evenings in romantic restaurants, drinking dry white wine and holding hands by candlelight. Unfortunately, after you're married, you won't be able to afford those fancy restaurants or have time for long, dreamy dinners.

Since I am a humor columnist, you might think I am biased, but I believe the most important question you must ask is: Is he *fun*? Do you laugh a lot? Do you have a lot to say to each other? I hate it when I go into a restaurant and I see a couple having dinner in pained silence. My beautiful young bride and I talk constantly, and laugh, too!

However, now that I have brought up the subject of my lovely wife, I realize that I probably would not have done well with these questions. I would have failed a husband assessment. I am not good with power tools, I don't make those super big bucks, I am a golfer, and I can't remember the last time I brought her flowers.

Thank goodness she didn't read this before she said, "I do."

Advanced Communication Systems

I don't know why technologists are working so hard to develop an instantaneous wireless communications system. It already exists. Not in any plastic wire-filled contraption but between old married folk! Any couple that has been together for five or more years has developed a communications system that AT&T, Microsoft, and Motorola combined would kill for. It has many sophisticated, futuristic features including:

Remote Communications: On his way home from the golf course, a man decides to stop at the supermarket to get hamburger, cheese, and buns. When he arrives home, he finds a note on the counter: "Let's have cheeseburgers for dinner tonight." How many computers do you know of that have this kind of advanced-needs-anticipation capability?

Nonverbal Communications: At a large crowded social event, one member of the team catches the eye of the other. No words or gestures are exchanged. A slight nod of the head is all that is required, and the two meet at the front door for departure. There were no prearranged signals, just an extraordinary communications system.

Abbreviated Communications: This team has also developed the ability to talk in shorthand. A conversation will go like this:

He: "Yardarm time?"

She: "Indeed, no fruit."

Translation:

He: "The sun is over the yardarm. I am going to have a drink. Are you interested?"

She: "Yes, I'd love a martini, thank you. No olives or lemon."

An outsider would have difficulty breaking this code. One word like "Puppy?" can be translated into a long sentence: "Did you feed the puppy, walk her, and put her in her pen?" No question, it is hard to match this system for speed and efficiency.

Early Warning System: A man at a social event runs into a cute young thing with a very short skirt. He starts a conversation with her but keeps getting communication flashes from his partner. In the back of his mind, he hears: "I know what you are thinking, and I don't like it. Move along, fella. Go talk to that guy in the corner about baseball."

Simultaneous Communications: The couple runs into an individual in the supermarket, and the man draws a total blank on the name. The woman says: "Darling, you know Joe Smith, don't you?"
The man replies: "Of course I do, dear," but inside he is thanking the great communications system for saving him again.

Communications Block: No network is complete without an advanced blocking system to filter out extraneous communications. In this scenario, the man sitting on the couch watching sports can automatically say, "Yes, dear," a dozen times but not receive or register any communications from the other party. This is when the wife will pass on information about upcoming commitments, reminding her husband later: "I told you Saturday while you were watching the Yankees, and you agreed!"

All those fancy companies are out there spending millions of dollars on market research, studying radio bands, microwave channels, and the like, but they are ignoring the most sophisticated system there is. Eat your heart out Blackberry and Treo. You can't beat an old married couple for advanced communications!

Herb's Guided Tour of the Empty Nest

I was having lunch the other day with the mother of two teenagers who was stressed out with all the pressures of being a parent. I commented that one day they would be grown up and gone. This seemed like a distant dream to her, and she said, "I wonder what it would be like."

Well, being an empty nester, I can tell her, and you, all about it. Here are just a few of the changes that will occur when your kids have flown the coop:

1. There will be room to park your car in your own driveway. No longer will there be a million cars parked everywhere (including on the lawn). Nor will there be cars constantly coming and going at all hours of the day and night.

2. The phone will not always be busy or ringing. You will be able to actually use the phone when you want and answer it when it rings, because there is chance the call might be for you. Previously, your offspring considered your use of the house phone to be a nuisance to them, as it interfered with their ability to talk endlessly with friends.

3. There will be no cans, containers, and food boxes left all over the house. The empty Coke can and half-eaten bag of corn chips will no longer rest on the TV stand; the day-old pizza box and beer bottle will not be stuck under the coffee table in the playroom.

4. You will be able to watch whatever TV shows you want. MTV will not be playing all the time, and you won't walk into the TV room and find a bunch of bodies draped everywhere—on couches, on the floor— watching an old horror movie or football game.

5. When you go to the grocery store, the bill will be $100 instead of $400. You'll probably need only one small handbasket instead of two family-size shopping carts. And despite the fact that you

have been spending $400 at the supermarket on a regular basis, you will not have to hear the kids complain that "there is nothing to eat" in the house.

6. You will also discover that there'll be room in the refrigerator for your food. The leftover Chinese containers, the cans of Slim-Rite and the diet sodas will no longer take 100 percent of the available space in the fridge. Actually, you will begin to stock up on food you like and not food requested by offspring and their friends.

7. Cash outflow will be dramatically reduced. "Cash outflow" is the discharge of those miscellaneous ten- and twenty-dollar bills you hand out for "gas" or "spending money" above and beyond established allowances. Once you're an empty nester, requests for distribution of funds will come via the telephone and the mail. These requests will be more substantial but less frequent.

8. The stress and strain on the clothes washer, the dryer, and the person responsible for doing the laundry will be substantially reduced. There won't be a three-foot-high pile of clothes always waiting to be washed or folded, and the machines won't run constantly, day and night. Instead of taking days, doing the laundry will take an hour or two.

9. Ditto for the dishwasher. You'll only need to run the dishwasher every third day, as opposed to three times a day. No longer will dirty plates and dishes be left in the sink, piled high toward the ceiling–if they are, you know who to blame.

10. The bathroom will always be available–and so much cleaner, it is unbelievable! No longer do you have to knock on the door and negotiate for time to take a shower or get ready to go to work.

11. You will not be forced to listen to rap music or hard rock at earsplitting volumes 22 hours a day (nor will you have to wear earplugs). This applies to your house, your car, the yard—everywhere. And no more starting the car after they've been driving it and getting blasted out by the noise. Until they leave, there are always loud screeching sounds around; after they leave, you will relish the quiet.

12. You will not trip over sneakers as you walk around the house. There won't be clothes left lying on the floor everywhere, waiting for an adult to pick them up, or empty milk containers in the refrigerator.

13. It will not seem as if there is always a party going on at your house. There won't be people sleeping over all the time, or frequent houseguests showing up for breakfast or dinner.

14. You will not have to lie awake at night, listening for the sound of the car in the driveway or the telephone call saying they are safe and spending the night at Tom's house. You will not have to negotiate curfews or appropriate clothing for a date.

15. In general, the activity level and the noise level in the house will be less. The video store won't call to say that you have five movies overdue (movies that you have to search for and ultimately find under a pile of dirty clothes). No one will try to borrow your car for a Saturday night. Video games won't be pinging all day long.

Becoming an empty nester requires some adjustment, though. Before they leave, you will be worried about how you're going to handle the void and the quiet. Then you'll feel guilty because you enjoy the empty nest so much. You and your spouse will actually be doing things like going on dates together. The final adjustment is that you will begin to look forward to having them home again, having the cans and sneakers left around and the loud music and the cars in the driveway.

One thing won't change, however. You will still worry. About driving. About drinking. About what they're eating and more. Even if they are not at home, you will always be a parent.

Don't Ask!

There are some questions a woman should never ask a man.

These are not silly questions; they are usually sensible, logical inquiries. The reason the questions should not be asked is that no man has a sensible, logical answer.

For example, a woman should avoid asking, "Why did you drop your underwear on the floor?" If asked this, a man will look at her with a puzzled expression on his face. He won't understand what is wrong. He has always dropped his underwear on the floor. Where else should it go? If a woman should ask, "How could you step over that pile of dirty clothes without picking it up?" a man will respond, "What pile?" There is no point inquiring about the dirty socks. Men think that they always get left by the side of the bed.

Another no-no question is: "Why do you have so many baseball hats?" The man will begin mumbling about needing different hats for different occasions; how certain hats are good for golf, and some are not, and he will try to explain how one is a lucky fishing hat, and how he has a sentimental attachment to another. A man should never have to defend the number of baseball hats he owns.

And of course, a woman should never ask, "Can I wash your baseball hat?" The man will instantly cry out, "No!" and then try to explain how a hat will lose its character, how the brim will lose its shape, how the color will change, how the hat won't be the same. Sometimes when one of his baseball caps gets especially smelly, a woman will sneak it into the washer while a man is at work, so she knows none of the above is true.

Another question a woman should avoid is, "Can I throw out those old sneakers?" Now, talk about a dumb question. Of course you can't! There is nothing worse than wearing new white sneakers. Those smelly things with the holes in them are perfectly broken in. A woman doesn't appreciate how long it took to get them that way. This also applies to T-shirts. To a man, a faded, ripped shirt is just perfect.

A woman should never ask, "Why are you going to the hardware store?" Ladies, ladies, ladies! Please don't ask that. A man goes to the hardware store because it's there. He will mutter something about needing a reverse decentralizing wrench with a zero-gravity handle, but you know that he already has three reverse decentralizing wrenches. For men, a hardware store is Mecca. They go to pay homage to an entire store full of tools and knickknacks. He'll come home with something he's bought, whether he needs it or not! (That's something you would never do, right?)

Other ix-nay questions revolve around the TV. A female should never ask, "Can I turn off the TV? You've been watching sports all day. When will I get some peace and quiet?" Or worse, "Can I hold the clicker?"

Men don't understand the concept of "too much TV," especially when there is another sports event that can be watched. He is in nirvana when there are three or four sports contests going on at once and another channel is showing a risqué movie. Then he can click back and forth furiously, getting the good parts of all the action. For a woman to ask if she can control the clicker is the ultimate power play by the opposite sex. A real slap in the face. It would be total humiliation for a man to give up the TV controller to a woman, who probably doesn't know how to operate it expertly.

The ultimate question a woman should never ask a man is, "Did you find it?" Of course he didn't find it! He's a man. He can't see things right in front of his nose. He will tell you there is no mustard in the refrigerator, that he searched high and low, but you easily find two jars. He can't locate the tape measure in the drawer, but you find it in two seconds. He's blind, like the rest of his gender.

So, ladies, you need to be careful about what you ask your man. If he puts his sweater back in the closet, don't ask if he put it away in the right spot. Don't ask if he folded it correctly. You know the answer. He didn't fold it. He shoved it in the nearest empty space. He's a man.

Day Bird and Night Owl

It's surprising that my wife and I get along so well, considering that I am an A.M. type, and she's a P.M. type. Or another way to put it: I'm a morning person, and she's an evening person, and never the two shall meet!

There is no question I'm an A.M. type. When I open my eyes in the morning, I am wide awake and ready to go. I pop out of bed all cheery and talkative, ready to accomplish a million tasks. I catch the 6:14 a.m. train each day, work out in a gym, have breakfast, and am still at my desk before 9 a.m.

My wife, on the other hand, needs two cups of coffee to get the right eye open and two more for the left. Her idea of a perfect morning is to sleep late, then lie in bed dozing for an hour or two before moving slowly downstairs for her first cup of coffee; this is followed by a long browse through the paper with a second cup of coffee and, eventually, getting dressed.

She accuses me of ricocheting off the walls in the morning. She says I am going 190 miles per hour when I wake up. She grumbles that there is no rational reason for a person to be that pleasant that early.

I have learned not to try to communicate with my wife in the morning. If I go in when she's asleep and ask a simple question, like, "Have you seen the checkbook?" the response I get is a low-pitched growl and a baring of teeth. I know if I shake her shoulder and repeat the question, there is a good chance I will lose my arm.

Therefore, our marriage continues on good terms as long as we don't try to communicate in the mornings. I try to be as quiet as possible as I shower and dress. Then, as I go out the door, I whisper, "Bye, dear," and run for the car. Only when I get the car rolling down the driveway do I think I've escaped another day.

Evenings, however, are a different matter. Just as my engine is running out of gas, I hear the sound of an Indy motor revving up, about to hit peak speed, and I know my wife is getting ready for "the best part of the day."

Now, my friends know I'm not exactly a sparkling person at night. I frequently fall asleep at dinner parties, sometimes before dinner is served. I cannot read at night at all. Half a page is enough to make the eyelids drop. (As a matter of fact, I go backward! I get into bed and can't remember where I was in the book, so I flip back a few pages and then fall asleep. The next night, I get into bed, flip back a few pages, and on it goes!). After 9 p.m., I am your basic vegetable.

As you can imagine, this makes for interesting marital confrontations. I am ready to leave the average dinner party around 7 p.m. Unfortunately, most evenings out don't start until after that time. My wife is the exact opposite. The longer the party goes, the happier she is.

One source of stress is our nightly TV routine. I normally get in bed in time to watch the ten o'clock news. I think the news lasts an hour, but my portion of it normally lasts fifteen minutes or less. When I start to snore, my wife gets up to turn off the TV, which wakes me up instantly. I insist I wasn't sleeping but really watching the news; yet two seconds after we get resettled with the TV going, I start snoring again. My bride occasionally asks me if I do this purposely to torture her, but I reply, "No, I just like watching the news at night."

There are some benefits to being different types, however. Whenever we have to go somewhere in the early morning—like a vacation or an airport trip—I'm always the one who gets everybody up and off. Then, in the evenings—when my wife is wide awake and the life of the party—she's able to explain to everyone why her husband is facedown in the soup, sleeping.

Although there might be a few minor short-term difficulties in our situation, the future looks great. As I get older, fatter, and more tired, I sleep later. Since I have less energy overall, I am less bouncy in the morning. Although my wife is still young, thin, and pretty, she is also going to bed a little earlier. Her howls at the moon don't last as long as they used to. If we keep going this way, in a few years, neither of us will be A.M. or P.M. types. We'll both be napping on the couch at noon.

Of Course

I've come to really distrust the expression "of course."

You're probably thinking that Foster has finally lost his marbles (of course). But I want you to stop for a moment and consider the phrase. Is it an expression that says exactly what it means? I don't think so.

Let me give you some examples.

There were four of us out to dinner the other night. At the end of the meal, two of us ordered decaf coffee and one ordered high-test. When the waiter came out with the three coffees, there was no marking to indicate which was which. After he tried to give me the regular (and I told him I'd ordered decaf), he simply spun the tray around, and put the cups in front of everyone. I asked him: "Are you sure I got the decaf?" His answer was, "Of course."

Now, I was more than a bit confused by the little shell game he played, so the "of course" didn't do much to build my confidence. I went home wondering if I was going to lie awake all night hating a waiter.

The next day, I went to the car-repair shop. Among other jobs I asked them to do was rotate the tires. When the bill came, there was no reference to the rotation on it, so I asked the service manager about it. He didn't even look at the bill or check with anyone. No, he says: "Of course they did it. If you asked them to do it, they did it."

Now, I hate to be skeptical, but I have almost zero confidence in his "of course." I don't know about your car dealership, but mine does not like to do work for free. I'm certain if they had rotated and balanced the tires, it would have been on the bill. Again, I went home thinking the work hadn't been done.

I looked up "of course" in the dictionary. *The American Heritage Dictionary* says it means "without any doubt, with certainty." Well, I have to tell you, I think it has exactly the opposite meaning. When people say "of course" to me, I am full of doubt. It is definitely not certain.

When your kid signs up for a fifty-mile charity bike-a-thon, you ask: "Are you sure you can go that distance?" The response from your offspring, who spends most of the day eating and sleeping and hasn't biked twenty feet in the last year is, "Of course!" How can you doubt him?

Here's another example. We get a leak under the sink, so I get out my collection of wrenches to work on it. When my wife asks me if I know what I'm doing, I look at her with a surprised expression on my face. I'm hurt that she would even ask. (She's challenging my manhood.) I say, "Of course I know what I'm doing." The truth of the matter is I have no clue. I'm hoping that brute force and dumb luck will fix the thing. As I say "of course," I am thinking that there is better than a fifty-fifty shot that we will need a plumber very shortly.

You see, I think people use the phrase "of course" when they are not 100 percent positive and when they are bluffing. "Yes" is a direct, positive answer. "Of course" is a little more vague and inexact. It leaves the responder with wiggle room.

Some people repeat the phrase, and this just makes matters worse. They say, "Of course. Of course." as if to double-emphasize the surety, but for me, they are only doubling the doubt. Sometimes, they accompany this with a dismissing wave of the hand. Well, as far as I'm concerned, their double positive is a double negative, plain and simple. I showed this to my son after I had finished writing it, and I asked him if he liked it. His answer?

"Of course!"

How to Be a Lousy Boss

I have just left the corporate world and gone into business for myself. While I miss the idea of a steady paycheck every Friday, there's one thing I really don't miss at all—having a boss! While every boss I've had has been great, I have watched a lot of horrendous bosses in action over the years. Actually, I have observed so many bad bosses that I've decided I could write a book on how to be a lousy boss."

If you want to qualify as the worst boss of the century, here are some of the techniques you need to master:

1. Resist the urge to say "thank you" or "good job." When an employee turns in an outstanding report, say something like, "It's about time." Or better yet, say nothing and flip through it.

2. As an offshoot of #1, don't ever say positive things about an employee in public. It is perfectly all right to say negative things and tell jokes about an employee's mistakes to a large group, but never anything that might be construed as praise.

3. If an employee completes a strong report that might impress the boss, take the work and pass it on in such a fashion that you will get credit for it. On the flip side, if you make a mistake, figure out a way to blame an employee for the screwup. Clearly, you do all the great work and make no mistakes.

4. If an employee begins to demonstrate competence in a job and gets to the position where he might be considered for promotion, change his responsibilities quickly. If an employee gets too good at their job, he might be a threat to you. You don't want to be in a position to have your work compared to someone else's.

5. When you give a project to a subordinate, be unclear about what you want. Don't ever put instructions in writing. The less specific you are, the

better the chances that what the employee delivers will have no connection whatsoever with what you wanted. In addition, you will have a ready-made opportunity to scold the employee.

6. If you have a large project that must be ready in time for the next day's 7 a.m. meeting, wait to give it to the employee late in the day so that he or she will have to work well into the evening to finish it. If the employee is truly dedicated, she shouldn't mind working till midnight. You, of course, can go home at 5 p.m., as always.

7. If an employee has several projects, don't prioritize them. This way, the person has absolutely no idea which to work on first. If an employee has numerous large projects, give him more work. You know what they say: "If you want something done, give it to a busy person!"

8. It is important that an employee not understand the reason why she's working on a project. She should never be told about the strategic implications of a job. She should just "do what she is told." Don't hold staff meetings and don't set goals and objectives for your staff. Keep them guessing!

9. When an employee has a large project to do, constantly interrupt him to "see how it's coming." Ask for interim reports that do nothing but impede the progress of the project.

10. Discourage informal gatherings of your staff (they might talk about you) and any occasion where they might laugh or have fun. On the other hand, you should demonstrate that you are a fun guy by telling crude, off-color jokes in mixed company whenever possible.

11. Keep accurate records of every mistake an employee makes. Keep track of every minute he is late to work or late back from lunch. It is probably best to keep a stopwatch so you can record the tardiness in minutes and seconds. Be especially persnickety about personal days and sick days, and don't forget to demand that letter from the doctor.

12. Keep this list of mistakes and absenteeism secret until it is performance-review time, and then spring it on the employee. Give her a poor performance rating and a minimal salary increase. Tell the

employee she is lucky to get any increase at all. Tell her she is lucky to have a job and lucky to have a boss like you to watch out for them. It is acceptable to brag about how large an increase you got to all your employees, or better yet, complain loudly about the level of taxes you must pay on your huge bonus.

Of course, when I was a boss, I didn't demonstrate any of these qualities. At least that's what my employees told me during performance-appraisal times.

On the Downward Slope

At some point in our lives, we reach the top of the hill. Actually, very few of us realize it when we have reached the plateau. It is only with hindsight that we see we are on the downward slope.

In an effort to help people make this determination, I hereby point out a few hints. If you find these statements to be true, there is a possibility that you are "over the hill."

• When you go out for the evening, you like being home by 9:30 p.m.

• You no longer care if your shoes are fashionable. What's really important is that they're comfortable.

• Tight-fitting underwear is no longer becoming or sexy.

• When you make a dinner reservation, you make it for 6:30 or 7 p.m.

• When traveling, you have a heightened awareness regarding the location (and distance to) the nearest bathroom.

• When you play golf, you find an excuse to take a golf cart instead of walking.

• You hesitate before ordering spicy food, wondering if it is going to upset your stomach and keep you awake all night.

• Lately, your favorite evening is staying home and renting a video or DVD. Then you fall asleep halfway through it.

• Instead of bending over to tie your shoes, you sit down and prop your shoe on a table.

• Advil is your friend.

• You have given up trying to remember phone numbers or dates. You write everything down, then search for hours trying to find the piece of paper with the information on it.

• Several well-meaning friends have explained the importance of getting a colonoscopy "at your age."

• Big snowstorms are no longer fun.

• When you purchase clothes from a catalog, you order "relaxed fit."

• Among the CDs you have in your car is at least one of the following artists: James Taylor, Simon & Garfunkel, or Bob Dylan.

• Before sports, you put several rubber contraptions and braces on your knees or elbows—or both.

• The balance in your IRA is becoming significant.

• You have a little shelf filled with vitamins, herbal supplements, and pills that you take on a regular basis.

• Your children and your friends' children are getting married. Now you can experience the joys of grandchildren.

• You don't have the latest digital music player and would have no idea how to operate it if you did. You have given up all hope of being on the cutting edge of technology.

• No one thinks of you as a "party animal." Doing shots and staying up to 3 a.m. are very distant memories.

• On a Saturday afternoon, you prefer to be at home, in a horizontal position on the couch.

• Either you use hair coloring or you look "distinctive."

• When heavy labor is required, you look to hire someone to do the work.

• You (men) no longer dream of having "six-pack abs." Instead, you just want to be able to see your feet when standing up.

• Your eyes are fine—except for small print, for things far away, or things near, or at night. You have found that bifocals are very handy (once you get used to them).

• You leave plenty of time to get to the airport or the doctor. No longer are you comfortable racing around to arrive on time for an appointment.

• The boy at the movie theatre automatically assumes you qualify for the senior-citizen rate.

• You walk into a room and then can't remember why.

• As the years go by, it becomes harder and harder to lose weight.

• You hate the new music, the new movies, the new plays, and are always remembering fondly how "it used to be."

• Every day, you sound more and more like your parents.

The final proof that you have hit the back nine is that you dread birthday parties. You don't see birthdays as cause for celebration. They are simple reminders that you are on the downward slope.

Actually, dear reader, even if you are not on this downward slope, you are most definitely at the end of this book.

COSIMO-on-DEMAND
NEW YORK

COSIMO is an innovative publisher of books and publications that inspire, inform and engage readers worldwide. Our titles are drawn from a range of subjects including health, business, philosophy, history, science and sacred texts. We specialize in using print-on-demand technology (POD), making it possible to publish books for both general and specialized audiences and to keep books in print indefinitely. With POD technology new titles can reach their audiences faster and more efficiently than with traditional publishing.

> ➤ **Permanent Availability:** Our books & publications never go out-of-print.

> ➤ **Global Availability:** Our books are always available online at popular retailers and can be ordered from your favorite local bookstore.

COSIMO CLASSICS brings to life unique, rare, out-of-print classics representing subjects as diverse as *Alternative Health, Business and Economics, Eastern Philosophy, Personal Growth, Mythology, Philosophy, Sacred Texts, Science, Spirituality* and much more!

COSIMO-on-DEMAND publishes your books, publications and reports. If you are an Author, part of an Organization, or a Benefactor with a publishing project and would like to bring books back into print, publish new books fast and effectively, would like your publications, books, training guides, and conference reports to be made available to your members and wider audiences around the world, we can assist you with your publishing needs.

Visit our website at www.cosimobooks.com to learn more about Cosimo, browse our catalog, take part in surveys or campaigns, and sign-up for our newsletter.

And if you wish please drop us a line at info@cosimobooks.com. We look forward to hearing from you.

YES	NO
	7/11/10 STEPH SAID TOMORR
	7/12/10 - SHE LIED.
	7/13/10 - NO RESPONSE
	7/15 - UGHH! SHE SAID

Printed in the United States
67490LVS00002B/205-249

9 781596 057746